Plantation Feasts and Festivities

A Celebration of the Grandes Dames of Virginia Food and Hospitality

by

Angela Mulloy

Foreword and Commentary by
Edna Lewis

Photographs by Shawn Green
Food Design by Douglas Gibson

Published by

The Court Wayne Press

in cooperation with

Montpelier

Home of James and Dolley Madison

Shawn Green, Photographer,
has a Bachelor's of Fine Arts from
Rochester Institute of Technology
and has a penchant for excellence. He has been
commissioned to photograph various subjects for
corporations and publications since 1988.
He lives in Richmond, Virgnia.

Douglas Gibson, Chef and Food Designer,
has been at the forefront of developing Virginia
regional cuisine for the past 15 years. His innovative
cuisine features new approaches to many of the
dishes he remembers from his childhood. As general
manager of Willow Grove today, he works with the
chefs to create similar regional dishes.

Published in the United States of America by
The Court Wayne Press
Post Office Box 19726
Boulder, Colorado 80308-2726

International Standard Book Number 1-57098-403-4
Library of Congress Catalog Card Number 00-109774

To the memory of my mother,
Clara Rhoades Ciccotelli,
who instilled in me a thirst for
knowledge, beauty, and perfection;
a passion for cooking, entertaining,
and all things treasured;
and a love for food, wine, and people.

Acknowledgements

First of all, many thanks to my dear friend, Edna Lewis, for the time she has spent helping us, for the recipes and support she has given us, and for the wealth of knowledge she has shared with us. Her philosophy of cooking has influenced us every day and in every way. We are indeed privileged to have her as a friend.

Thanks, too, to all the homeowners—the Honorable Helen Marie Taylor, Mrs. Molly Barrow, Mr. and Mrs. William Collier, Mr. and Mrs. Pendleton Bresee, Dr. and Mrs. Dennis Campbell, Mr. and Mrs. Chester Nagle—who graciously allowed us into their homes to take photos for this book.

To my friend and colleague, Doug Gibson, for his wonderful recipes, the hours upon hours he spent preparing the food and designing its presentation, and his loyal friendship for more than a decade.

Shawn Green for his undying excellence, enthusiasm, and energy in taking these beautiful photographs of the homes and the food.

Randy Huwa and Lee Langston-Harrison of the Montpelier executive staff for their assistance in gathering information and checking the accuracy of my data and Ann Miller for her book, *Antebellum Orange*, which provided the historical data for the Madison houses.

Jennifer Green for lending her husband to me for the many weeks it took to photograph the subjects for this book and for the time she spent refining the typography and design.

Jackie Howell for her many suggestions on content, validating historical data, and meticulous proofreading of the final draft.

John Graves for lending us his marvelous vintage Rolls Royce, and Mary Collins Jones and Connie Dulaney for their wonderful suggestions and providing many of the beautiful accessories.

And, last but certainly not least, my heartfelt thanks to some very special people who have influenced my life and professional standards more than they will ever know:

Gerry Davis, for her friendship and for everything she has done for me over the years, which is far too much to list here.

Alan Voorhees, who made this all possible by backing his faith in me with support for Willow Grove.

Walt Hansen, my friend and mentor, for his encouragement and support in everything I have done, or tried to do, over the past 30 years.

My daughter Lisa, son-in-law Michael, and grandchildren, Bobby, David, Stephanie, and Christopher, for their love, loyalty, and endless hours of help at Willow Grove.

And, of course, Richard, who puts up with me no matter what mood or world I happen to be in at the moment.

Contents

Foreword

I have fond memories of Orange County, Virginia, where I was born and grew up more than 80 years ago. I lived with my parents and grandparents on a working farm not far from Montpelier and the other plantations in this book. Although I now live in Georgia, I try to return home several times a year to work with the chefs at Willow Grove. We have been developing dishes together since they asked me to be the guest chef at a celebration of Thomas Jefferson's 250th birth anniversary nearly ten years ago. With nut trees, berries, and wild greens all around Orange County, it was easy to create period menus and special dishes from records available through local history groups in the area. The result is a collection of Southern specialties that blends into the history of the plantation.

The recipes blend old classics and new twists on traditional themes. Some are tried-and-true creations from our personal collections, some are recreations of early recipes, and some are traditional renditions of family favorites. All, however, have been developed for a special occasion, for those times when you want to indulge. Therefore, we took no shortcuts in preparation of ingredients. We did not want to compromise when it came to taste.

Modern machinery and new methods have made life on the farm much easier, but it is still possible to take pride in a job well done and celebrate the season's bounty. Such it is, too, with food. Though many techniques have been replaced by new ones, it is still possible to connect with the land and prepare fresh food that explores and preserves these old traditions. This book recalls fond memories of the good food and good times of my childhood and brings back the legacy of the Old Virginia I remember.

Edna Lewis

Edna Lewis at Willow Grove.

Preface

The idea for this cookbook was conceived as a result of numerous requests and encouragement to share the treasure trove of culinary, historical, and cultural heritage in Orange County, Virginia. Each chapter contains menus and recipes for recreating seasonal celebrations that took place on the antebellum Virginia plantation, many of which still continue today.

This book has been written from the heart, for I have been immersed in a wondrous love affair with Orange County since our serendipitous meeting in 1987 when I discovered both Willow Grove Plantation and Dolley Madison. The similarities were uncanny.

Born in Philadelphia and transplanted to Orange, I was amazed to learn that Dolley had lived in Philadelphia and moved to Orange. I lived in New Jersey, just a few miles from Haddonfield where Dolley visited her uncle who owned an inn there. Willow

Grove was a suburb of Philadelphia that I frequented as a child. And I saw in this Willow Grove the opportunity to open an inn, which by definition is based on hospitality.

It was here at Willow Grove that I had the good fortune to meet and become friends with Edna Lewis. Known throughout the country as the Grand Dame of Southern Cooking, Edna has been sharing with us her recipes, techniques, experiences, and recollections of growing up here in Orange County. For the past ten years, I have been compiling her comments and hints, as well as the recipes she has shared with us.

It seemed fitting, then, to include them, along with quotes from Dolley Madison's letters, in this book to celebrate the 250th anniversary of the birth of James Madison, native of Orange and Father of our Constitution. Famous for her outreaching hospitality, his wife Dolley was a master at entertaining. And since the foundation of entertaining is good food, Edna and Dolley seemed a perfect match to present the food and celebrations of the Virginia plantation.

This book has been written imaginatively, with an eye toward creating a blend of food and traditions, those small parcels of culture that combined to form the plantation. The recipes presented are those that have been developed by the Willow Grove chefs over the years, those which have been in our families for years, and those that Edna has given us to use when she joined us as guest chef for our many events.

All recipes have been carefully tested and modified to today's methods so that you will find them easy to follow. And while we have endeavored to provide explicit instructions for their preparation, we have assumed a basic understanding of and finesse with cooking. Therefore, we did not include instructions for such basics as roasting meat, blanching vegetables, deglazing a pan, caramelizing sugar, or testing a cake for doneness. And, since it is almost impossible to give exact measurements for some ingredients, many recipes call for a dash of this or a pinch of that.

The recipes have been adjusted to serve six to eight adults, and they assume that only the freshest, purest ingredients will be used: fresh herbs, kosher salt, freshly ground or cracked pepper, sweet butter, heavy cream, stone-ground cornmeal, reduced stocks. We have carefully selected the ingredients to bring the great taste of plantation dishes into your home. All the ingredients called for are readily available in most supermarkets or gourmet shops. But don't be afraid to experiment or substitute if you can't find something.

The table settings suggested in each chapter reflect my love for collecting treasures that make dining a unique experience. Each depicts a certain mood and a particular style. But there are as many good styles as there are personalities, so don't hesitate to express your own ideas. Let your imagination soar. And have fun. The key to entertaining now, as it was centuries ago, is to create and enjoy.

I hope you will enjoy trying these recipes and that the dishes you create will bring much happiness to you and those you love. Please let me have your comments and suggestions. We welcome and encourage them.

Angela

Introduction

Orange County, named in honor of William, Prince of Orange, served as the impetus for westward expansion. In 1710, Lieutenant Governor Alexander Spotswood led an expedition over the Blue Ridge Mountains to publicize the fact that the mountains were passable and rich lands lay beyond. One of the men on that expedition, Colonel James Taylor II, established a successful plantation which included much of what is now the Town of Orange. He reared a large family on that plantation, and two of his great-grandsons, James Madison and Zachary Taylor, became early Presidents of the United States.

As each of his children married, Taylor subdivided the original grant into smaller estates for their homes. These estates provided the land for Montpelier, the lifelong home of James Madison, and the homes of his siblings and cousins. It is these homes, and the homes of the Madisons' friends, that inspired this book. Built by craftsmen who had been employed by Thomas Jefferson in the construction of the University of Virginia, many of these homes have Jefferson's distinctive Classical Revival style. And all of them were owned by people who entertained and visited James and Dolley Madison.

James and Dolley Madison lived in Orange County before, during, and after his presidency. The Madisons were friends with most of the landowners in Orange County, and James had multiple ties with his kin. The couple is known to have visited the homes of the Taylors, the Barbours, the Conways, the Clarks, and the Willises, all owners of plantations featured in this book.

The Virginia Plantation

The Virginia plantation was a miniature society, a world of its own. Completely self-sufficient, its success depended entirely on the land and those who worked it. Planters raised crops for their own use, for cash, and for trade. Their blacksmiths made tools to plow the land. Their carpenters and masons built barns of timber, stone, and clay. Their pigs filled the larder; their cattle provided skins; their sheep furnished wool. They had cooks and bakers to prepare meals, spinners and weavers to make blankets and clothing, cobblers to make shoes and saddles. Except for a few luxury items, the plantation furnished everything. And everyone had a specific role.

The manor house was the center of this small universe, and situated around it was a whole set of buildings: schoolhouse, spring house, weaving house, ice house, smoke house, ash house, barns, and stables. The kitchen, usually a short distance from the manor house, was filled with cookware and other essentials of food preparation. It was in this kitchen that all the roasting, broiling, boiling, and baking were done. It was here that the plantation workers had free reign, where they could express themselves fully, where they excelled. It was here that Southern cooking had its true beginning.

Virginia planters were country gentlemen. They directed and managed their plantations with taste and finesse. They loved the countryside, and they loved to work the land. But they also loved horse racing, cockfighting, and fine wine. And, above all, they

Plantation children were schooled in an antebellum schoolhouse much like this one at Willow Grove.

loved to entertain, which they did frequently.

Gracious hospitality soon became the custom of the day. Friend or stranger was invited to dine, to stay a night, a few days, a few weeks. People came from near and far to join in the hunt, enjoy an elaborate dinner, or attend a fancy ball. Festive parties were held in mansions, formal teas on verandas, lavish picnics in cool woods, barbecues by rivers and streams.

However, though the planter was manager of the cash crop, it was his wife who was the center of the household. She, not the planter, was the real focus of the plantation. It was she who made the plantation famous for its hospitality. It was she who ruled the household. And it was she who managed the kitchen. But it was the enslaved kitchen workers who developed the recipes and created the feasts that made the plantation famous for its food.

Delightful Dolley

For half a century, Dolley Madison was one of the most important women in the social circles of America. She entertained everyone with a kindness and affection that was part of her nature. To this day, she is remembered as one of the best known and best loved hostesses—America's first First Lady. Her early childhood, however, belies her later years.

Dolley was born in North Carolina on May 20, 1768, to Quaker parents, who soon moved to Virginia where they enjoyed the lifestyle of wealthy Virginia plantation owners. As Quakers, the Paynes believed that slavery was wrong, but at the time it was illegal to free slaves in Virginia. However, in spite of the consequences, they were among the first Quakers to sacrifice their comfortable life-styles. When Dolley was 15, the Paynes abruptly freed their slaves, sold their holdings, and moved to Quaker-dominated Philadelphia, the stronghold of their religion.

As a Quaker, Dolley led a rather somber life in Philadelphia. However, it is believed she found respite by traveling

This portrait of Dolley Madison, by G. Kazigan after Gilbert Stuart, is displayed at Montpelier.

to her uncle's popular tavern in nearby Haddonfield, New Jersey, which may have inspired her culinary acumen and social graces. She enjoyed interacting with her gregarious aunt and uncle and likely spent time in the kitchen, which was noted for serving the best food in the area. And although her Quaker upbringing prohibited her from dancing, Dolley delighted in the social excitement of the tavern's frequently hosted music and dancing fests.

Exceptionally pretty with a natural vivacity, she had a magnetic personality that made her the center of attention even as a teenager.

When Dolley was 22, her uncle sold the tavern. She married Quaker lawyer John Todd and they soon had two children. Tragically, both her husband and her youngest child died in a yellow fever epidemic that raged through Philadelphia in 1793. That same year, she met James Madison who was immediately taken by the young, vivacious widow with laughing blue eyes. Married the next year, they became soul mates. "Our hearts understand each other," she is known to have told him.

Expelled from the Society of Friends for marrying outside the faith, Dolley discarded her somber clothing. She ordered dresses from Paris, selecting only the finest of fashions. Her high-waisted dresses with plunging necklines attracted the interest of social writers during the period. Thus, she became America's first fashion celebrity—a leader in dress design and fashion,

James and Dolley Madison used this "Old Paris" porcelain during his years as Secretary of State and President.

setting trends in both America and Europe.

Her social graces made her famous. She warmly welcomed everyone with a hospitality that combined the new Republican spirit with the old-fashioned elegance of rural Virginia. She served as unofficial First Lady for widower Thomas Jefferson during her husband's term as his Secretary of State. And,

when Madison became President, she presided over the first inaugural ball, becoming the unquestioned center of Washington society. Widely known for her legendary Wednesday night receptions, she smoothed many a tension between intense party rivalries.

Her genius as a hostess was also reflected in the warmth of her home. The first to decorate the President's Mansion, she chose appointments that completely dazzled her guests—French chairs, Sevres porcelain, enormous gilded mirrors, colorful carpets, lush silk damask draperies, gleaming mahogany tables, and the finest paintings and sculptures. And against this backdrop of magnificent furnishings were huge bouquets of flowers from her gardens.

Both in Washington and at Montpelier, hospitality became a Dolley Madison tradition. She gladly welcomed politicians, diplomats, envoys, warrior chiefs, family, friends, and even travelers she didn't know—sharing her table, offering a bed, providing conversation and entertainment to all alike.

James and Dolley lived in retirement at Montpelier. Dolley, known for her vivaciousness and eloquence, entertained there frequently. Relatives and friends from far and near came to visit, and Dolley received her guests with overflowing kindness and affection. After the death of her beloved husband in 1836, she returned to Washington where she spent her last years as a leading hostess in Washington. At her funeral in 1849, President Zachary Taylor eulogized that she was truly America's first lady.

Dolley Madison is fondly remembered throughout the nation for setting the tone for Washington society. But here in Piedmont, Virginia, she has been immortalized for her parties in every season—teas and picnics in the spring, lawn parties and barbecues in summer, hunt breakfasts and harvest dinners in the fall, and holiday parties and balls in the winter. And she is loved by all, not only as the doyenne of Washington and the mistress of Montpelier, but as the woman who reflected Virginia society with her gracious entertaining—a careful blend of European formality and American simplicity.

Spring

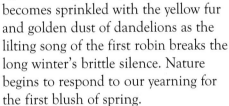

On the plantation, the year begins in spring, a time of rebirth and renewed activity. The gardens and ponds begin to come to life after their winter rest. Crocuses, marsh marigolds, and early bog primulas peep their heads out of the ground, blooming as harbingers of spring. The meadow becomes sprinkled with the yellow fur and golden dust of dandelions as the lilting song of the first robin breaks the long winter's brittle silence. Nature begins to respond to our yearning for the first blush of spring.

Plantation families knew always when winter was over. Even though some cold days and a wet snow might yet come, everyone knew that the trees would be budding any day and that thawed streams would be rising on delicate watercress edges. Soon the earth would be warm enough to plow and after-dinner conversation would turn to the crops that would need planting in the weeks ahead.

In Virginia, the first of the spring's bounty were the salsify and parsnips left in the ground from fall. They were soon followed by wild asparagus, poke, wild mustard, wild strawberries, and of course, watercress, that welcome treat of spring.

Then came the famous garden peas. They were considered a real delicacy—the highlight of the season—and we couldn't wait for them to ripen. These peas were tender and flavorful, and we loved to eat them. Since they only lasted about two weeks, we had to pick them as soon as they were ripe. This was a big job, so all the neighbors helped pick; then we all shared them.

Shad, the first fish to appear in spring, were just about the only fish we ate. Since they were gone by summer, we couldn't get enough of them while they were in season. We were usually too excited to wait for dinner, so we ate the fish for breakfast.

We then looked forward to a dinner of the first chickens from the spring hatching. It was a real treat. Our chickens were all fed by hand and were especially tender. They were delicious pan-cooked.

Edna Lewis

An Early Easter Supper

Ushering in the spring time is Easter, when the lovely, soft greens of spring appear on trees, birds begin their serenade, and bees nuzzle in the blossoms of the lilac bush. Rivers and streams overflow with the melting snows of winter. Tarragon, thyme, and mint begin to peep through the earth. Bleeding heart blossoms nod their heads in the gentle breezes. Azaleas and spring bulbs bloom in profusion. What a wonderful time to invite friends to enjoy an early supper featuring fresh herbs and vegetables.

After an egg hunt, an informal supper is set out in the garden. The abundance of flowers inspires the decorations, and the delightful fresh colors of early spring are brought to the table. Diminutive cowslip, primroses, crocuses, violets, and forget-me-nots fill tiny Spode demitasse cups at each place setting. Small wooden eggs with hand-painted folk designs sit naturally in a shallow basket along with speckled and softly tinted farm fresh eggs.

A collection of heirloom Spode complements the pale colors of the eggs and the fresh colors of the early spring flowers. And the menu reflects the best of the new spring growth: shad roe and lamb, new asparagus, baby beets, and the first watercress of the season.

Nineteenth-century hand-painted Pennsylvania chairs surround a table set for an al fresco Easter supper.

Greenfield

Set in a private park amidst towering osage orange trees, magnificent boxwood, and perennial gardens, Greenfield lies unnoticed by neighbors. The current house was built in the 1830s by Thomas Scott. It is two stories high over an English basement and laid in Flemish bond with brick made on the property. The interior has original pine flooring, six fireplaces, windows with some hand-blown glass, and fine molding throughout. A covered arcade leads to the guest house, formerly the kitchen, which contains three ovens in the basement.

The Palladian portico and kitchen wing were added in the early 20th century. A host of outbuildings, perhaps from the 18th century, survive. They include a brick-lined circular icehouse, double privy, a "pit" greenhouse, office, rebuilt smokehouse, and corncrib.

The original house was built in 1729 by James Taylor, 2nd, and his wife Martha Thompson after deeding their original home, Bloomsbury, to their eldest son, James Taylor, 3rd. James and Martha Taylor were the great-grandparents of two American Presidents, James Madison and Zachary Taylor.

The senior Taylor died at Greenfield at age 55 and his wife with their many children, including the heir, Erasmus, continued in residence until her death in 1762.

The parents were buried in the family graveyard on the property. Their grandson, James Taylor, the son of Colonel George Taylor of Midland, also lived on the property and was clerk of Orange County from 1772 to 1798. The county records were kept in the office at Greenfield.

An Early Easter Supper

Menu

Planters Punch

Minted Sweet Green Pea Soup

Blue Cheese and Pecan Wafers

Citrus Watercress Salad

Sautéed Shad Roe

Pan-Roasted Rack of Lamb

Salsify Cakes

Orange Rosemary Baby Beets

Cheese Popovers

Strawberry-Rhubarb Pie

Easter

The feast of Easter was named after the Anglo-Saxon goddess of spring, Eostre, whose festival was celebrated at the vernal equinox. Its date was set in the year A.D. 325 by the Council of Nicea, which decided that Easter should fall on the first Sunday following the first full moon after the vernal equinox. The feast was well established in Europe by the second century, but it was not until the Civil War that the message of Easter began to be expressed in this country. Since then it has become a major springtime celebration that is a secular, as well as religious, celebration.

Many of Easter's customs are pagan in origin and have nothing to do with religion. Like all festivals of ancient origin, Easter is closely tied to nature; hence, the symbolic use of eggs and the Easter rabbit. Its joyous customs delight children and adults alike.

EARLY SPRING PEAS WERE FLAVORFUL AND TENDER. WE SERVED THEM WITH LOTS OF BUTTER AND CREAM.

Edna Lewis

Planters Punch

There are several variations to the original Planter's Punch, which was first concocted in the Caribbean. This version includes bourbon, which was probably added when the drink was brought to Virginia.

1 liter light rum	2 ounces bourbon
1 pint dark rum	1/4 teaspoon curacao
1 lime, juiced	Orange slices
1/2 lemon, juiced	Maraschino cherries
1/2 orange, juiced	Sprigs of mint
1 teaspoon pineapple juice	

Combine juices, light rum, and dark rum. Pour into 16-ounce glasses filled with shaved ice. Stir until glass is frosted. Add bourbon and top with curacao. Decorate with orange, cherry, and mint.

Minted Sweet Green Pea Soup

Sweet tender garden peas give this soup a flavor that is entirely different than that made from dried peas. It is delicious served hot or cold.

1-1/2 pounds fresh green peas
4-1/2 cups water
1/2 cup chopped mint
1/2 teaspoon black pepper
Salt

Heat water to boiling. Rinse, drain, and shell peas. Stir in mint, pepper, and salt. Cook uncovered for about 15 minutes, until peas are tender. Add salt and correct seasoning.

Blue Cheese and Pecan Wafers

The tang provided by the blue cheese makes these delicate wafers a perfect complement to the soup.

2-1/2 cups all-purpose flour
1-1/2 teaspoons salt
8 teaspoons butter
12 ounces blue cheese
1 cup pecans, chopped

Cream butter and cheese. Add dry ingredients. Add nuts. Stir to mix well. Form into 1-inch balls. Flatten each ball with palm of hand. Bake at 375 degrees for 10 minutes.

Blue cheese and pecan wafers are a tasty appetizer before dinner.

Citrus Watercress Salad

This salad is best prepared with wild watercress, which has a more peppery flavor than that found in the grocery store.

For the salad
6 bunches watercress
2 oranges
2 blood oranges
Freshly cracked black pepper

For the dressing
1/4 cup lemon juice
1/4 cup orange juice
1 lemon, zest only
1 tablespoon sugar
1/2 tablespoon salt
1/2 cup olive oil

*I*MAGINE, IF YOU CAN, A GREATER TRIAL TO THE PATIENCE OF US FARMERS THAN THE DESTRUCTION OF A RADIANT PATCH OF GREEN PEAS BY FROST!

Dolley Madison

Wash watercress and remove thick stems. Allow to dry. Peel and section oranges. In a mixing bowl, combine lemon and orange juices, salt, sugar, and lemon zest. Whisk, adding oil slowly, until well combined. When ready to serve, mix watercress and citrus sections and toss with dressing. Garnish with freshly cracked black pepper.

Sautéed Shad Roe

Shad roe, which appears in Virginia only in spring, was historically served along with the fish. However, since shad is very bony and hard to prepare, it has fallen out of favor in modern times. The roe, a prized delicacy, is tender and moist when prepared simply.

WE ALWAYS SERVED THE ROE WITH THE SHAD, WHICH WE COATED WITH CORNMEAL AND FRIED UNTIL IT WAS CRISP.

Edna Lewis

8 slices thick bacon	Salt
8 single shad roe	Freshly ground black pepper
8 tablespoons unsalted butter	1/4 cup fresh lemon juice

Wrap the shad in bacon and secure with toothpicks. Put the butter in a heavy frying pan and heat until very hot, being careful that the butter doesn't brown. Season the roe with salt and pepper and put in pan. Slash slightly to prevent the roe from blistering. Reduce the heat and cook for about 5 minutes. Turn and cook another 5 minutes. Do not overcook. The roe should be pink inside. Remove roe from pan and remove toothpicks. Pour a little lemon juice over each piece.

Pan-Roasted Rack of Lamb

In the 18th- and 19th centuries, a roasted leg of mutton would have been served as only older sheep were butchered. Lambs were either sold or kept for their wool.

1 cup dry bread crumbs	6 lamb racks
1 cup salted peanuts	Salt and freshly ground pepper
1 teaspoon garlic, chopped	6 teaspoons Dijon mustard
1/4 cup olive oil	

Preheat oven to 450 degrees. Combine first 3 ingredients in bowl of a food processor. Process until fine. Set aside. Trim excess fat from lamb racks. Season with salt and pepper. Heat a frying pan until it is very hot. Put a little olive oil in the pan. Oil should move in pan and smoke a little at the edges. Brown lamb racks one at a time, turning to sear and seal all sides. Place racks in a large shallow baking pan and roast in oven for 5-10 minutes, depending on desired temperature. Remove racks from oven, brush with Dijon mustard and dredge in bread crumb mixture. Return to oven for about 5 minutes. Let rest 5-10 minutes before serving.

The Easter Egg Roll

The Easter egg games popular centuries ago are still delighting children today. A favorite game, brought to America by the English, has been rolling hard-boiled eggs on the lawn, crashing them into each other until only one unbroken egg remains. In England and parts of Europe, the eggs were rolled down a hill, the object being to roll as many as possible without cracking the shells.

The White House Egg Roll was started at the suggestion of Dolley Madison. Her son, Payne Todd, learned that Egyptian children rolled colored eggs on the site of the pyramids. He shared this idea with Dolley, who was fascinated by the custom. She thought it would be a fun game for the many children who visited her. She even dyed the eggs herself.

When she was First Lady, she let the children roll eggs on the lawn of the Capitol. The children would sit in rows holding baskets of colored hard-boiled eggs. Those children on the upper row would send the eggs rolling to the row below, who in turn would send them to the row below. This continued until the eggs reached the children at the foot of the hill, who would run to the top and start rolling the eggs down the hill again.

The game was suspended during the Civil War and discontinued in 1878, but it is said that a group of children marched to the White House, Easter egg baskets in hand, and President Hayes's wife allowed them to roll their eggs on the White House lawn. The tradition continued until World War I, when it was suspended once again. President Eisenhower permitted it to resume in 1953, and it has been held ever since.

This is truly a child's day. Adults are not permitted on the lawn unless they accompany a child. The eggs are rolled down a slight slope south of the Truman balcony. In the background, the military band plays. And, if she is in town, the First Lady may appear and mingle with the egg rollers, just as Dolley Madison did 200 years ago.

A perfectly cooked rack of lamb is served on an heirloom Spode plate.

Salsify Cakes

Be sure to keep the salsify covered with cold water as contact with the air will turn it black.

2 bunches salsify
2 tablespoons butter
1 teaspoon salt
Dash of pepper

2 tablespoons milk
4 tablespoons flour
2 tablespoons lamb drippings

Salsify was one of the first vegetables out of our garden. It was planted in early spring and left alone until the following winter when we would dig it up as soon as the ground thawed.

Edna Lewis

Scrape each root of salsify thoroughly and place in cold water. Grate and add butter, salt, pepper, and milk. Shape into cakes. Heat drippings until just smoking. Coat salsify cakes with flour and brown slowly in hot drippings.

Orange Rosemary Baby Beets

For the best flavor in this dish, look for tiny beets that have just been dug up. Be sure to cool the beets in their cooking liquid so they don't lose their color.

1 pound baby beets
1 cup water
1-1/2 cups fresh orange juice
1 tablespoon rosemary
Salt and pepper

Remove all but one inch of beet tops. Place beets in saucepan with one cup of water and boil until tender. Cool in cooking liquid and slip off skins. Chop rosemary and whisk together with orange juice. Season to taste with salt and pepper. Add beets to orange juice mixture and marinate for 48 hours. Serve at room temperature.

Fresh orange zest provides contrasting color to the beets.

Cheese Popovers

Be sure to leave the oven door closed to give the popovers a chance to puff up. The sides of the popovers should be firm and crusty before you remove them from the oven or they will collapse.

4 eggs
2 cups milk
1/2 teaspoon salt
2 cups sifted all-purpose flour
2 tablespoons unsalted butter
1/2 cup grated cheddar cheese

Beat eggs lightly. Add milk and mix well. Add the salt to the flour and add slowly to the egg mixture, stirring constantly. Cover and set aside to rest for at least one hour. Lightly grease muffin tins with unsalted butter. Put muffin tins in 425 degree oven and heat until hot without burning the butter. Remove muffin tins from the oven and fill each pan 2/3 full with batter. Sprinkle each with cheese. Bake for about 25 minutes without opening the oven door. After 25 minutes, if popovers are not brown and crusty, bake for another 5-10 minutes. Serve piping hot.

I EXPECT A LARGE PARTY TO FILL THE HOUSE NEXT WEEK.

Dolley Madison

Spode demitasse cups make interesting holders for tiny bouquets of spring flowers.

Onion Skin Eggs

Decorating eggs with onion skins is a centuries-old German folk tradition. It has been passed from generation to generation by Pennsylvanians of German origin and was brought to Virginia with the Germanic settlement in the 18th century. Germans in Pennsylvania and Virginia continue to make these eggs to give as gifts on Easter.

It takes about six cups of yellow onion skins to dye a dozen or so eggs. Eggs and onion skins should be placed in a very clean saucepan, covered with water, brought to a boil very slowly so that the eggs do not crack, and then simmered for five hours. Eggs should be turned periodically using a wooden spoon, and water should be added as necessary. The eggs will turn a deep mahogany.

Once the eggs are cool, a pin, razor blade, or other small sharp object can be used to scratch designs in the eggs. Traditionally, the designs were similar to graffito, the designs put on pottery by the Pennsylvania Dutch. The deeper the scratch, the whiter the design.

Traditionally, eggs were wiped with vegetable oil, but spraying with several light coats of varnish will make them more durable. Periodic rubbing with vegetable oil will revive the deep color.

The Easter Parade

The custom of the Easter parade began nearly 2,000 years ago. One belief is that Emperor Constantine commanded his council to wear more elegant robes to celebrate the Resurrection. Another is traced to the early era when white robes were conferred on the recently baptized, and regular members of the church wore new attire in remembrance of their earlier baptisms. A third is simply that new clothes were worn to signify the beginning of the new year, which then began in March.

In antebellum days, it was believed that good luck would be ensured by wearing an article of clothing for the first time on Easter. The practice of donning new clothes led to the idea of parading in them, and late in the 19th century the Easter parade became a favorite pastime. People in every state gathered to watch the parades of gaily dressed ladies, wearing hats trimmed with spring flowers and bright ribbons, strolling home from church.

A lattice crust gives a strawberry-rhurbab pie a special touch.

Strawberry-Rhubarb Pie

Cut up on the stalks of the rhubarb as the leaves and root are not edible. Select very firm strawberries to prevent their breaking up.

For the pastry
2 cups all-purpose flour
1/4 teaspoon salt
1/2 cup butter
1/3 cup ice water

For the filling
1 cup sugar
1/4 cup all-purpose flour
1/4 teaspoon salt
2 cups diced rhubarb
1 pint strawberries, halved
2 tablespoons butter

Preheat oven to 425 degrees. Put flour and salt in a medium bowl. Add butter and cut in with pastry blender until consistency of coarse meal. Add ice water a little at a time, stirring with a fork until the dough leaves the side of the bowl. Form a ball and cut into two pieces. Roll out one piece about 1/8-inch thick. Place in 9-inch glass pie pan and set aside. Mix sugar, flour, and salt together. Put rhubarb and strawberries in a bowl and sprinkle with sugar-flour mixture. Put into pie shell and dot with butter. Roll out second piece of dough and place on rhubarb mixture, cutting a few slits in the top to let steam escape. Or, for a prettier pie, make a lattice top by cutting dough into strips and weaving on top of the rhubarb mixture. Trim edges and flute. Bake for 35-40 minutes, until top is nicely browned.

A Garden Tea

A balmy spring day is an auspicious time to gather for afternoon tea and a welcome break in the middle of a long day. It is a splendid opportunity for relaxed, quiet conversation with family and friends. It's a chance to bring out the fine silver, crisp linens, and heirloom china. And it's a marvelous way to entertain when lunch is too informal and dinner too extensive. The combination of food, conversation, and ambiance of a garden tea can be the passport to a different time and place.

As early as the Colonial period, tea emerged as a ceremony. It was a popular way to entertain friends and give them a moment away from the spinning world. Here we recreate a late afternoon tea for members of Orange County's Garden Club. Tables are dressed with antique linens. Sheffield silver tea services are filled with a variety of aromatic teas. And delectables are set out on lovely hand-painted Limoges china with its universally popular pink roses.

There couldn't be a more perfect setting for a tea. A serene terrace. A Victorian garden alive with the blooms of spring bulbs, ancient boxwood, and budding magnolias. It's a scene that evokes the genteel era that preceded the turn of the century.

Antique Limoges china and Sheffield silver make an elegant table for tea when set out on heirloom lace.

Frascati

Frascati sits behind a circular driveway surrounded by immense, centuries-old boxwood. A massive arched front door opens to a monumental entry hall surrounded by hand-carved cornices. Its lovely, large dining room is on view from the immense reception hall, signifying immediately that food has always been an important part of entertaining here.

Built in 1823 by Philip Barbour, brother of Virginia Governor James Barbour, Frascati stands as a reminder of the 18th-century fashion for giving plantations romantic Italian names. The house, built in the Jeffersonian Classical style, stands much as it was built. Two stories high over an English basement, it has a pedimented portico and a hipped roof. Though its plan is a conventional two rooms on either side of a large hallway, the workmanship is outstanding.

The brickwork, laid in Flemish bond, is said to be the finest in the area. Original woodwork includes the wainscoting, the stairway, the Classical mantels, the front doorway, and arch in the hall, which was once faux marble that resembled cut blocks of polished stone. The current owner stripped away a portion of the wall to showcase this magnificent artwork. The parlor boasts plasterwork that has no rival. Rich moldings surround the room, and a large plaster medallion takes center stage on the ceiling.

The gardens were originally enclosed by serpentine walls similar to those at the University of Virginia and the house was surrounded by numerous dependencies. Unfortunately, the only dependency that remains is a brick kitchen, whose fine workmanship leads one to believe that this was a most elegant plantation.

A Garden Tea

Menu

Potted Virginia Trout

Crumpets

Currant Scones

Sally Lunn Tea Cakes

Wild Strawberry Jam

Assorted Tea Sandwiches

Mini Chocolate Coffee Walnut Muffins

English Shortbread

Pound Cake Clara with Lemon Creme

Raspberry Sherbet

Potted Virginia Trout

The English high tea always included some variation of potted meat. This updated version using local trout gives the dish a Virginia twist.

1 pound fresh boned trout fillets
1/4 cup water
1/2 cup softened butter
1 lemon, juice only
1/2 teaspoon mace
1 bay leaf
Salt and pepper

Lay fillets in a single layer in baking pan. Disperse herbs, water, lemon juice and butter over fish. Cover and poach for about 10 to 15 minutes, until flesh is opaque and flaky. Skin trout and break into small pieces. Puree in food processor with butter and seasoning. Adjust seasoning and pack into attractive china container. Chill. Serve with crumpets or thinly sliced bread.

Tea is at its best when served in a beautiful Limoges cup.

FRUIT BUTTERS ARE EASY TO MAKE AND ARE A DELICIOUS TOPPING FOR THESE CRUMPETS. SIMPLY MASH THE FRUIT INTO THE BUTTER AND PUT IN A RAMEKIN.

Edna Lewis

Crumpets

Crumpets should be eaten fresh and hot; however, they can be toasted if they are left from the day before. They are delicious with the potted trout.

2-1/2 cups all-purpose flour
1/2 ounce yeast
1/2 teaspoon sugar
1-1/3 cups warm water
3/4 cup milk
1/2 teaspoon baking soda
1 teaspoon salt
Oil or shortening

Sift half the flour in a bowl. Add yeast, sugar, and water and blend until smooth. Leave in a warm place for about 20 minutes or until frothy. Add 1/2 cup of the milk and remaining ingredients. Beat well, adding more milk if needed to make a thick batter. Grease a griddle and plain metal cookie cutters. Arrange rings on the griddle and heat thoroughly. Pour about 2 tablespoons of the batter into each ring and cook for about 10 minutes, until they are set and bubbles appear. Turn over and remove the rings. Cook for another 10 minutes. Repeat with remaining batter.

Tea as an Institution

Tea, first introduced to England in the mid-17th century, reached national prominence by the 18th century. Legend has it that Anna, Duchess of Bedford, introduced the idea of afternoon tea to England in the early 19th century in an effort to stave off her hunger between meals. As the time between breakfast and dinner lengthened in the summer, it is fabled that this lady took to her bedroom in mid-afternoon and demanded that her servants bring her tea, bread, and sweets. She soon acquired the habit of taking afternoon tea and began introducing it to her friends. Thus a ritual was born.

Much of the credit for popularizing tea, however, must also be given to Josiah Wedgwood, a potter from Staffordshire whose pieces were so reasonably priced that almost everyone was able to own an elegant tea service. His first teapots were made of simple earthenware and salt-glazed stoneware. But they soon graduated to Queensware, his invention of an extra fine creamer, and finally to his famous Jasperware, molded white classical figures on unglazed, usually blue, earthenware.

A 19-century Baltimore Hepplewhite sideboard is set for tea with heirloom Rosenthal cups and sterling silver.

The British government saw the popularity of tea as an excellent source of revenue and imposed taxes that kept its price exorbitantly high. But when England attempted to tax the colonies, the Americans rebelled. And in 1773, at an enormous fancy dress tea party held in Boston, Americans denounced tea in favor of independence.

With considerable embellishment, the Victorians elevated tea to a high social occasion. Although the family tea, often the last meal of the day, was usually a homey affair that could be expanded to accommodate friends who might stop by, the formal tea party required guests to wear their best clothing and the hostess to bring out her fanciest lace, gleaming silver tea service, and most elegant china.

Though afternoon tea suffered a decline after World War II, it has felt a resurgence in the past few years. Americans are once again finding the values in the ceremony of tea as a culinary and social event. It has a calming effect that is important in today's hectic world. And it brings people together for a brief hour of pleasure.

Currant Scones

To be at their best, scones should be baked and served fresh from the oven.

4 cups all-purpose flour
1-1/2 teaspoons baking soda
1 tablespoon cream of tartar
1/4 teaspoon salt
1/2 pound butter
1 cup currants
1 egg, beaten
1 cup buttermilk
2 egg yolks
2 tablespoons water

Preheat oven to 425 degrees. Combine first four ingredients in a mixing bowl. Cut in butter until mixture resembles cornmeal. Add currants, beaten egg, and enough of the buttermilk to make a soft dough. Knead lightly until ingredients are just combined. Roll out to 1/2-inch thickness. Cut into half moons and place on greased baking sheets. Combine egg yolk and water and brush on each scone. Bake for 12-15 minutes until golden brown.

*I*F YOU CAN FIND WILD STRAWBERRIES, YOU WON'T BE DISAPPOINTED. NOTHING CAN MATCH THEIR FLAVOR, AND THEY COME UP IN THE SAME SPOT YEAR AFTER YEAR.

Edna Lewis

Wild Strawberry Jam

Wild strawberries make the best jam by far, but if they are not available, try to find small cultivated berries without much pith.

5 cups wild strawberries, sliced
3 cups sugar
2 tablespoons orange peel, grated

Combine all ingredients in a large saucepan. Slowly bring mixture to a boil and cook over medium heat until sugar is completely dissolved. Cook for about 45 minutes, stirring frequently to prevent sticking. Pour mixture into sterilized jars and refrigerate.

Currant scones in an antique silver biscuit box sit on a vintage Battenburg lace tablecloth.

Sally Lunn Tea Cakes

This is a rich, slightly sweet bread that doesn't require kneading even though it contains yeast.

For the cakes
4 tablespoons butter
3/4 cup milk
1 teaspoon sugar
1 tablespoon active dry yeast
2 eggs, beaten
3 cups all-purpose flour
1 teaspoon salt

For the glaze
4 tablespoons sugar
4 tablespoons water

Place sugar and milk in a saucepan, add butter, and heat until butter is melted. Cool slightly. Sprinkle yeast over mixture and let sit in warm place for 10 minutes until mixture is frothy. Beat in eggs. Sift flour and salt together in large bowl. Add liquid mixture and mix well. Turn out on lightly floured surface and knead lightly for about 10 minutes. Shape into 12 balls and place in greased muffin tin. Place tin in an oiled plastic bag and let rise in a warm place for about 1 hour, or until dough fills the pan. Bake at 450 degrees about 20 minutes, or until golden brown. Turn out on wire rack. Make glaze by mixing water and sugar together. Brush over tops of cakes while they are still warm.

A beautiful silver samovar makes an elegant tea service presentation.

I DRANK TEA WITH THE FINGEYS AND MRS. FOREST, THE AMOUNT OF VISITS ACCOMPLISHED.

Dolley Madison

Homemade Tea Breads

Although making bread can be time-consuming, it is well worth the effort, as there is nothing better than a sandwich made with homemade bread.

YOU CAN ALSO MAKE NICE CRISP DINNER ROLLS WITH THIS RECIPE. JUST PUT A PAN OF WATER IN THE BOTTOM OF THE OVEN AND BAKE THE BREAD AT 375 DEGREES.

Edna Lewis

For the country white
1 quart warm water
3-1/3 pounds bread flour
2 tablespoons salt
2 tablespoons active dry yeast

For the farmhouse wheat
3/4 quart warm water
1-1/3 pounds wheat flour
1-1/3 pounds all-purpose flour
1-1/2 tablespoons salt

1-3/4 tablespoons dry yeast
3/4 cup honey

For the old-fashioned rye
6 cups high-gluten bread flour
2 cups coarse rye flour
4 teaspoons caraway seeds
2 tablespoons active dry yeast
2 tablespoons sea salt
2-3/4 cups water

Generously grease loaf pans and set aside. In the mixing bowl of an electric mixer, combine all ingredients in the order they appear above. Using a dough hook, mix on low speed for 12 minutes. Remove dough hook and cover bowl with plastic wrap. Set aside in warm place and let rise until doubled in bulk. Remove dough from bowl and split into three equal portions. Place each portion of dough into a loaf plan and cover each with plastic wrap. Allow to rise again, this time for about 30 minutes. Bake at 350 degrees about 30-35 minutes or until a dark golden brown.

Making homemade bread is fun and rewarding.

Tea Sandwiches

The secret to making beautiful tea sandwiches is to trim and slice the bread very carefully.

Trim crust from three loaves of bread and cut each loaf into thin slices. When sandwiches are made, place on barely damp tea towels and cover with more damp towels until time to serve. To serve, arrange sandwiches on silver platter. Garnish with fresh flowers, herbs, or carved vegetables.

Cucumber Sandwiches

2 cucumbers
Salt
1 tablespoon olive oil
1 tablespoon lemon juice
1 teaspoon sugar
White pepper
1 loaf wheat bread
1/2 cup soft butter

Using a food processor or mandoline fitted with a metal blade, slice cucumbers into very thin, transparent slices. Lightly salt slices, place in a colander, and weight with a plate. Let stand for about 2 hours, pressing out juice from time to time. Combine with oil, lemon juice, sugar, and white pepper. Spread two slices of bread with soft butter. Place two layers of cucumber on the bread and top with a second piece of bread. Press down lightly with palm of hand. Cut into triangles.

Chicken Sandwiches

6 whole breasts of chicken
1/2 cup mayonnaise
1/2 cup sour cream
1 cup celery
1/2 cup pecans
1/4 cup golden raisins
2 tablespoons curry powder
Salt and pepper to taste
1 loaf farmhouse wheat bread
Fresh herbs for garnish

Poach chicken breasts and let cool completely. Remove skin and bones from chicken breasts and cut into small pieces. Finely chop celery, pecans, and raisins and add to chicken. Add curry powder and mix gently. Mix together mayonnaise and sour cream and stir into the chicken a tablespoon at a time, mixing with a fork until creamy. Cut thin slices of bread into quarters. Spoon a small amount of salad on the bread. Garnish with fresh herbs.

Radish Sandwiches

1 crusty baguette
1/2 cup softened butter
1 bunch fresh radishes
Kosher salt

Slice baguette and spread slices with softened butter. Slice radishes very thin. Lay radishes on buttered bread slices. Sprinkle each slice with kosher salt.

Watercress Sandwiches

1 large bunch watercress
1/2 cup butter
2 tablespoons Dijon mustard
1 loaf rye bread

Cut coarse stems off watercress. Wash watercress and dry thoroughly. Whip butter and Dijon mustard together. Butter two slices of bread and pile watercress onto one slice. Place other slice on top. Cut sandwiches in half, letting the green leaves burst out.

Cream Cheese Sandwiches

1/4 cup fresh herbs
1 cup cream cheese
2 tablespoons heavy cream
1 loaf country white bread
1 pint alfalfa sprouts

Finely chop fresh herbs. Put cream cheese and cream into bowl of electric mixer and beat until smooth. Stir herbs into mixture. Spread herbed cream cheese on one slice of white bread. Top with sprouts and second slice of bread. Continue until entire loaf is used. Cut out sandwich rounds using biscuit cutter.

Historic Garden Week

Historic Garden Week is one of Virginia's most beautiful events. Countless garden clubs have expended their energies toward the beautification of Virginia's towns and cities, and the fame of their projects has spread. Today, Historic Garden Week is a well-known and popular endeavor. Each April, people travel from all parts of the country to savor the splendor of a variety of flowering gardens. Formal gardens enchant the eye. Cottage gardens entice the palate. Herb gardens tickle the nose.

It is uncertain whose idea it was to organize the first garden club, but toward the end of the 19th century, local garden clubs developed profusely. These clubs were small and exclusive by design. Membership was by invitation only, and invitations were offered only to the landed gentry.

Plantation manor homes were natural garden club meeting sites. They had both the beautiful gardens and the staff necessary for projects and study. Meetings blended Robert's Rules of Order with gossip, plant exchange, and poetry readings. A pink tea usually followed, with everything in shades of pink—plates, cups, linens, and even the sherbet.

MR. MONROE AND FAMILY DINED WITH US YESTERDAY IN A LARGE PARTY GIVEN TO MR. JONES.

Dolley Madison

Mini Chocolate Coffee Walnut Muffins

These rich muffins are more like cupcakes and would make a delicious luncheon dessert or snack.

1 cup butter
1 cup brown sugar
1 cup white sugar
5 tablespoons instant coffee
4 teaspoons vanilla
4 eggs

1-1/3 cups milk
3-1/4 cups all-purpose flour
1 teaspoon salt
2 tablespoons baking powder
1-1/2 cups chocolate chips
2 cups walnuts

Preheat oven to 350 degrees. Coarsely chop walnuts and chocolate chips. Cream sugars with butter, coffee, and vanilla. Beat in eggs. Mix flour, salt, and baking powder together. Add flour and milk alternately to creamed mixture, beating after each addition. Fold in chocolate and walnuts. Spoon into greased mini-muffin pans and bake for 12-15 minutes.

English Shortbread

Though not as rich as the traditional English or Scottish shortbreads, this is a perfect choice to accompany a cup of piping hot tea.

1 cup butter
1/2 cup sugar
1 egg
3 cups sifted all-purpose flour
1 teaspoon baking powder

Preheat oven to 325 degrees. Cream butter and sugar until fluffy. Sift together flour and baking powder. Add egg and mix well. Add dry ingredients to creamed mixture, stirring well. Knead dough lightly until it holds together. Roll out on floured surface and cut into 2-inch squares. Place squares on ungreased baking sheet and prick each with a fork. Bake for 12 minutes or until lightly browned.

*T*HE LARGE AMOUNT OF BUTTER IN SHORTCAKE IS WHAT GIVES THESE CAKES A CRUMBLY TEXTURE.

Edna Lewis

Raspberry Sherbet

Flash-frozen raspberries make a credible substitute when fresh raspberries are not in season.

5 cups raspberries
2 cups sugar
1 orange

Purée raspberries. Grate orange rind to yield 2 teaspoons. Combine raspberries, sugar, and grated orange rind. Mix until sugar is completely dissolved. Put mixture into ice cream freezer and freeze according to maker's instructions. Sherbet will take about 30 minutes to freeze. Keep container in freezer until ready to serve. Scoop into chilled cups or bowls and garnish with fresh raspberries or other fresh fruit.

Raspberry sherbet looks especially refreshing when served in etched crystal glasses on a Heisey plate.

A Proper Tea

Today, the afternoon tea need not meet any authenticity standards. It should, however, create a rich sense of period that transports guests to another era, away from the day-to-day world of practical concerns.

Offer delicate sandwiches made with an assortment of breads and variety of fillings, a selection of confections and desserts, and, of course, scones with jam. Substitute soft, whipped butter for the clotted cream, which is very hard to find in the United States. Heap the trays high to give the feeling of plenty. Include a variety of teas to allow sampling of different blends. And prepare the tea properly.

First turn on the cold faucet and let the water run a little to ensure the water will be full of oxygen to bring out the tea's best flavor. Then fill a kettle with the fresh, cold water and put it on the stove to boil. Do not overboil the water, or too much oxygen will escape and the tea will taste flat.

As soon as the water reaches a full rolling boil, brew and serve the tea. Prepare a silver tray with teapot, sugar, very thin slices of lemon, and milk. Place a napkin to the left of the tray.

Preheat an earthenware or china teapot by rinsing it with hot water. Swirl the hot water around a bit and then empty the water from the teapot. Using one heaping teaspoon of tea for each cup of water plus one teaspoon for the pot, add tea leaves to the pot.

Pour boiling water over the tea leaves and cover the pot. Allow small-leaf tea to steep about 3 minutes, large-leaf tea about 5 minutes. For a stronger brew, use more tea. Don't extend the brewing time or the tea will be bitter. Have a second pot of boiling water handy. If the tea is too strong, add a little of the hot water. If it is too weak, start again. Strain the brewed tea into another pot or cup. Serve immediately.

A Wedgwood Jasper cake cover adds subtle color to a tea table.

Pound Cake Clara

The preferred choice for every birthday in our home, this cake is much moister than a normal pound cake. It is equally good plain, iced, or with lemon cream.

3 cups all-purpose flour, sifted
4 teaspoons baking powder
1/2 teaspoon salt
1 cup butter

2 cups sugar
4 eggs, separated
1 teaspoon vanilla extract
1 cup milk

Preheat oven to 350 degrees. Sift together flour, salt, and baking powder. Cream butter and sugar until light and fluffy. Add egg yolks one at a time, beating after each addition. Add vanilla and beat until well blended. To butter mixture, add sifted dry ingredients alternately with milk, beginning and ending with the dry ingredients. Beat egg whites until stiff but not dry. Fold gently into batter. Pour into greased tube pan. Bake for 1 hour.

THE SECRET TO A GOOD POUND CAKE IS TO MEASURE THE FLOUR CAREFULLY, USE COLD BUTTER, AND BAKE IN A SLOW OVEN.

Edna Lewis

Lemon Creme

This is a perfect complement to the pound cake served without frosting.

5 eggs
1 cup sugar
1/2 cup butter

1 cup lemon juice
Peel of 1 lemon, grated
1 cup heavy cream

Combine eggs, sugar, lemon, butter, and lemon rind. Whip together. Place mixing bowl over simmering water and whisk constantly until mixture is creamy and thick. Allow to chill completely. Whip cream to soft peaks and fold chilled mixture into cream.

Pound cake Clara is served from an antique flint glass cake stand.

Dolley's Decor

When Dolley married James, her taste began to change. She grew to love French style. Shedding the simple furniture of her Quaker days, she began collecting French furniture. She called upon American diplomats stationed in Europe, such as James Monroe, to send furniture back to her. And she befriended the wives of French ministers who refined her knowledge of French high style.

Dolley decorated Montpelier and her Washington house on F Street with French appointments. She chose Louis XVI chairs, Sevres porcelain, rich carpets, and period mahogany tables acquired from auctions of the estates of nobles. She filled her rooms with an unbelievable gallery of museum-quality paintings and sculptures. And she set out enormous mirrors that reflected the large bouquets of flowers she adored.

Portraits, medallions, and other elements adorned the walls of the dining room at Montpelier. The large mahogany table and sideboard were heavy with silver accumulated by three families. The clock room, named out of respect for the old-fashioned English clock that had regulated the household for many years, was filled more than 50 statues, including those of Washington, Jefferson, and Adams. Persian carpets covered the floors; mirrors and pictures covered the walls. Despite the elegance and formality of the furnishings and appointments, Dolley's artistic combination of furniture, china, and books piled high gave her rooms a cheerful, homelike atmosphere.

A Madison-family chair sits next to an heirloom desk.

When James was elected President, however, she was faced with a dilemma. French furniture and extravagance were out of the question for the President's Mansion. Republicans, Federalists, and European diplomats all had to be appeased. And this required a careful blend of European style and American comfort. Dolley thus chose furniture, draperies, wallpaper, china, and crystal that presented an image fine enough for Federalist high fashion yet simple enough to soothe the more down-home Republicans.

Her choices were impeccable. High-quality American furniture manufactured by Baltimore, New York, and Philadelphia craftsmen who were the finest in the nation. Satin wallpaper and curtains of her favorite color "sunflower" yellow. Crimson upholstery for the drawing room. Portraits of the three former Presidents in the State Dining Room. The finest musical instruments. And three of the huge ornamental mirrors she dearly loved.

A Tailgate Picnic for the Races

Spring is the time the steeplechase comes alive. Peonies, long-favored by Virginians, make their appearance in the garden. Dogwood, iris, and larkspur soon follow suit and burst into bloom. With the hunt season recently ended, horse people in Piedmont Virginia turn their thoughts to races, picnics, and parties until the fall hunt season begins again.

These springtime events draw dressy tailgate picnickers, many of whom understand little about horses or racing. For them, it is enough that springtime is in full bloom and that the race is certain to guarantee them a good time. The event provides the perfect setting for a winning afternoon. The races are exciting. The mint juleps are plentiful. And everyone is hungry.

Tailgate picnics are elegant and extravagant. Wicker hampers brim with the first bounty of a new growing season: butterhead lettuce as soft as velvet, crunchy radishes full of spicy water, tender peppery arugula, red ripe strawberries, and the first morels of the season. Colors run the full gamut; flavors are honest and fresh. Set on a tailgate with Royal Doulton china, a more elaborate picnic would be hard to find.

A vintage Rolls Royce is ready for a tailgate picnic at Montpelier.

Montpelier

A *squirrel's leap from heaven* is how the Madisons described their much-loved Montpelier. From the front portico, Dolley would watch as the horse-drawn carriages came up the long, tree-shaded driveway. She made a point of having refreshments awaiting guests as they entered the reception hall, flooded in warm light from the glorious triple-hung windows facing the rear garden. Often, when it was cold and dreary, she would serve her guests hot bouillon as they arrived and before they left.

Granted to Ambrose Madison and his wife Frances, daughter of Colonel James Taylor II, in 1723, Montpelier was to become the lifelong home of their grandson, President James Madison.

Upon Ambrose Madison's early death, Frances ran the plantation until her son, James Sr., came of age. James greatly improved the property, increasing the family's holdings and presiding over the plantation. Soon to be President, James Jr. acquired the property upon his father's death. He continued to preside over the plantation where he practiced his lifelong interest in agricultural tech-

niques. It became a retreat from public life, and later a retirement home, for him and his wife Dolley.

Though James and Dolley were childless, they were surrounded by the huge families of their brothers and sisters. Feeling Montpelier to be home, the family came often and stayed long. James's youngest sister, Fanny, lived at Montpelier and, 23 years younger than her famous brother, was more like a daughter than a sister to James. Dolley's sisters, Lucy and Anna, her brother John, and their children also visited frequently. During his public service, Madison's visits to Montpelier were occasions for large family gatherings that often included more than a hundred relatives and friends.

Mount Pleasant, the original structure built by Ambrose Madison, no longer

stands, but archaeologists have identified what is believed to be the foundation of the home and its dependent buildings. The original section of the present house, built by James Sr. about 1760, was of brick construction in typical Georgian style—two rooms on either side of a central hall. Additional rooms were added in 1797, forming what could be termed the first duplex house. The elder Madisons lived on one side of the hallway, with James and his new bride on the other. James and Dolley made several renovations during the period 1809-1812, adding one-story wings, a front portico, a small rear porch, and the garden temple. Under this temple, which was well suited for reflection and reading, was an icehouse that enabled Dolley to serve chilled refreshments to their guests.

After changing hands six times in the 1800s, the home was purchased by William duPont in the early 20th century. He made extensive changes to the interior which now intermingle with those of the Madisons.

A Tailgate Picnic for the Races

Menu

Morel and Scallion Tart with Sweet Potato Crust

Baby Spinach Salad with Honey Walnut Vinaigrette

Herb-Crusted Beef Tenderloin

Vidalia Onion Marmalade

Grilled Bourbon-Molasses Glazed Quail

Wild Rice Salad

Herbed Sweet Potato Cakes

Fresh Asparagus with Creamy Lemon Dressing

Madison Cakes

Bourbon Walnut Chocolate Pie

Mint Juleps

Morels

One of spring's greatest treasures is the esteemed morel mushroom. Found in Virginia only during early spring, the morel grows in cool, moist shady places on the edges of forests. It fruits most abundantly on recently disturbed or cleared land, popping up under dead trees, wood chip mulch, and in abandoned fruit orchards. Finding a patch of morels is no guarantee, however, that they will be in the same place the following year as they enjoy a change of pace. But in the event the morel is found year after year in the same spot, the hunter will never tell a soul.

So sought after is this delicious fungus that its admirers will travel hundreds of miles in its pursuit. Blended into the forest's background, its dark triangle shadow mocks wood, bark, stone, and cone, making a keen eye and swift foot a prerogative for gathering this tasty reward.

I LOVE TO SERVE COOKED MORELS THAT HAVE BEEN MARINATED IN OLIVE OIL AND GARLIC. THEY HOLD UP TO THE OIL, AND THEIR FLAVOR IS ENHANCED BY THE GARLIC.

Edna Lewis

Morel and Scallion Tart with Sweet Potato Crust

It is important to use sweet potatoes, not yams, in this recipe. The flesh of the sweet potato is dry and cream-colored. The moist, dark flesh of the yam will impart a different texture to this crust.

For the sweet potato crust
3 cups sifted all-purpose flour
1 tablespoon baking powder
1-1/2 teaspoons salt
3 cups mashed cooked sweet
    potatoes
1 cup melted butter
3 eggs, beaten

For the tart
1/2 cup country ham
1-1/4 pounds morels
1 cup scallions, finely chopped
1-1/2 teaspoons thyme
1/4 cup butter
1 tablespoon dry sherry
1-1/2 cups heavy cream
1/4 cup grated Romano cheese

Mix together flour, baking powder, and salt. Make well in center of flour mixture and put mashed potatoes, butter, and eggs in the well. Mix thoroughly. Shape into a flattened ball and chill for at least 1 hour. Roll out on floured board and lay in 10-inch tart shell. Trim excess. Cut ham into strips and slice mushrooms. Combine with scallions and thyme. Sauté briefly in the butter. Add sherry. Cover and cook for about 2 minutes. Add cream and cook at high heat for about 5 minutes, until mixture is thick. Stir in cheese. Pour into sweet potato crust. Bake at 350 degrees for 30-40 minutes.

Baby Spinach Salad

Spinach makes a delicious salad, but it is very sandy. It should be washed a handful at a time to remove all traces of the sand.

1 pound fresh baby spinach
1 red onion
3 Granny Smith apples

Remove stems from spinach and wash thoroughly. Spin dry with salad spinner or let dry thoroughly on towels. Peel onion and slice into thin rings. Remove core from apples and slice into wedges. Mix onion rings and apple slices with spinach and toss with honey walnut vinaigrette.

An antique cruet sits next to ingredients for a baby spinach salad.

Honey Walnut Vinaigrette

Be sure to leave the walnuts in large enough pieces to provide a pleasant crunch to this salad.

1/2 cup walnuts
1 rib celery
1/4 small onion
1/2 small carrot
1 clove garlic

1 egg yolk
1/2 cup red wine vinegar
1-1/2 cups olive oil
1/2 cup warm honey
Salt and pepper

WE HAVE A CONTINUAL ROUND OF COMPANY.

Dolley Madison

Using a food processor, grind walnuts into small pieces. Remove from processor and set aside. Chop celery, onion, and carrot. Place celery, onion, carrot, garlic in processor and process until finely ground. Remove and set aside. Put egg yolk and vinegar in processor and process, adding oil slowly in a steady stream until mixture is emulsified. Add warm honey and process until well mixed. Add vegetables and pulse until well blended. Add walnuts and blend. Season with salt and pepper.

Herb~Crusted Beef Tenderloin

*C*OOKED UNTIL
CRUSTY ON THE OUTSIDE
AND RARE AND JUICY ON
THE INSIDE, THIS IS ONE OF
MY FAVORITE DISHES. A
BERNAISE SAUCE MAKES IT
EVEN MORE SPECIAL. JUST BE
SURE THE HERBS ARE NICE
AND FRESH.

Edna Lewis

The flavors of the garlic and herbs intensify as this beef cools. Serve at room temperature.

1 beef tenderloin, trimmed	4 leaves fresh sage
8 cloves garlic, slivered	4 sprigs fresh parsley
4 sprigs fresh thyme	4 sprigs fresh chives
4 sprigs fresh rosemary	1/2 cup oil

Prepare barbecue or gas grill. Peel and sliver garlic. Finely chop herbs together. Whisk together oil, garlic, and the chopped herbs. Rub the tenderloin with the mixture. Cut small slits in tenderloin with point of very sharp paring knife. Place a sliver of garlic in each slit. Allow beef to stand for 30 minutes. Place beef on grill over low heat. Turn often to avoid burning herbs and garlic.

Vidalia Onion Marmalade

These sweet onions are only available during spring and early summer, but this marmalade makes it possible to enjoy their flavor all year long.

2 tablespoons olive oil	1/3 cup red wine
2 Vidalia onions, diced	1/2 cup beef stock
1/2 cup brown sugar	Salt and pepper
1/3 cup balsamic vinegar	

Heat oil in skillet. Add onions and sauté until caramelized. Add sugar and cook for about 2 minutes, until sugar is well dissolved. Add vinegar and red wine and simmer for 5 minutes. Add beef stock and simmer until the liquid is reduced by half and the mixture is a thick pulp. Season with salt and pepper.

Vidalia onion marmalade looks tempting in a cut crystal jar with a silver top.

Grilled Bourbon-Molasses Glazed Quail

Quail can be purchased whole or boned in most specialty supermarkets. They are tender and delicious at room temperature.

6 quail
1/2 cup molasses
1/2 cup pure maple syrup
1 tablespoon bourbon
1/4 cup brown sugar
Salt and pepper

Mix molasses, maple syrup, bourbon, brown sugar, salt, and pepper in large bowl. Add the quail, turning to make sure birds are well coated. Marinate at least 8 hours. Grill the quail, turning often and basting with remaining marinade to produce a sweet, flavorful crust.

Grilled bourbon-molasses glazed quail are delicious served with herbed sweet potato cakes.

Wild Rice Salad

Although this is a simple and quick dish to prepare, wild rice— actually a grass and not a rice—will take about an hour to cook.

For the salad
1 pound wild rice
1/2 red pepper
1/2 green pepper
1/2 yellow pepper
1 small carrot
1/2 medium red onion
1 bunch scallions

2 tablespoons butter
Salt and pepper

For the dressing
1/2 cup olive oil
1/4 cup red wine vinegar
2 tablespoons sugar
1/2 cup chopped fresh herbs

Cook rice according to package directions. Allow to cool. Meanwhile, dice vegetables and sauté in pan over medium heat until tender. Mix with rice and scallions. Cool and add diced vegetables. Whisk together oil, vinegar, sugar, and herbs until emulsified. Add to cooled rice and vegetable mixture. Toss well.

*F*IFTEEN OR TWENTY OF THE FAMILY AND CON-NECTION DINED HERE . . .

Dolley Madison

The Steeplechase

The word steeplechase comes from the old custom of using a church steeple as the goal of a race. Originally run cross-country, the steeplechase incorporated natural obstacles such as brush, fences, and ditches. Today, the race is run on a flagged course of fence hurdles over which the horses leap with electrifying grace. As in the past, the steeplechase engenders parties, picnics, social events, balls, and other festivities.

Steeplechasing is for those who consider racing a sport. Compared to the more commercial flat racing, steeplechase purses are small, and the cash value is relatively unimportant. The cherished prize is a trophy, or sometimes only a ribbon, but the owners would not trade their collections for all the purse winnings in the country.

The rolling green countryside of the Virginia Piedmont has always been the perfect setting for the steeplechase. An annual springtime event, the steeplechase in Virginia has a camaraderie that makes race day a social reunion as well as a day of sport. It attracts thousands of spectators who make a day of the races, bringing elaborate picnics to spread on the lawn or arrange on tailgates.

Tables and tailgates are dressed to the nines: fine china and delicate crystal, crisp imported linens, heavy silver candlesticks, huge bouquets of fresh flowers. And the feasts that unfurl rival the best in Southern cooking. Often the day is topped off at a formal hunt ball at which men wear tuxedos, tails, or hunting pinques.

Wedgwood Cornflower earthenware, set on an antique Hepplewhite inlay game table, adds a special touch to a tailgate picnic.

Herbed Sweet Potato Cakes

Be sure to heat the oil to the smoking point so the potatoes fry quickly without becoming soggy.

2 medium sweet potatoes
1 medium white potato
1/2 medium red onion
1/2 cup scallions

4 eggs
1/2 cup sour cream
1/2 tablespoon chopped thyme
Salt and pepper

Peel and grate potatoes and finely dice onion. Chop scallions. Combine eggs, sour cream, onion, and scallions. Mix well. Add grated potatoes to mixture. Add salt, pepper, and thyme. Mix together. Heat a small amount of oil in a skillet until just smoking. Make small cakes from potato mixture and fry in oil until golden brown. Drain well on paper towels.

SWEET POTATOES SHOULD BE BOUGHT IN SEASON AND SHOULD NEVER BE REFRIGERATED AS THEY WILL LOSE THEIR FLAVOR.

Edna Lewis

Madison Cakes

It is believed Dolley served these tasty delectables, more a yeast roll than a cake, at both Montpelier and the President's Mansion.

2 medium white potatoes
1/2 ounce compressed yeast
1/4 cup lukewarm water
1/2 cup unsalted butter

2 teaspoons salt
2 tablespoons sugar
3-1/2 cups all-purpose flour

Boil the potatoes until tender. Strain and reserve 1 cup of the liquid. Peel and mash potatoes. In a small bowl cover the yeast with the lukewarm water. Let stand until dissolved. Melt the butter in a small saucepan. Put reserved potato water, mashed potatoes, yeast, and 1/4 cup melted butter into a large bowl. Add the salt and sugar and mix thoroughly. Stir in half the flour and mix. Add remaining flour a half cup at a time, mixing well after each addition. Turn the dough onto a floured board and knead until smooth and spongy. Return to a well-greased bowl. Cover with a damp cloth and let rise until doubled in bulk. Put remaining 1/4 cup butter in a clean bowl. Turn dough onto floured board and knead a few seconds. Cover and let rise 5 minutes. Make small balls out of dough and dip into melted butter. Put on baking sheet, cover, and let rise about 40 minutes. Bake at 375 degrees for about 30 minutes.

Madison cakes in a Wedgwood cornflower muffin dish sit on an heirloom quilt.

Asparagus with Lemon Dressing

There should be sufficient water clinging to the asparagus stalks to steam the asparagus. Be frugal if you must add more water.

Asparagus with creamy lemon dressing in a crystal dish.

2 pounds fresh asparagus
2 tablespoons butter
2 egg yolks
1/4 cup lemon juice
1/4 cup white wine
1 lemon, peel only

1 garlic clove
1 cup olive oil
2 tablespoons Parmesan cheese
1 tablespoon parsley, chopped
Salt and pepper

Wash asparagus in cold water. Place butter and asparagus in a skillet. Cover and cook until *al dente*. Combine egg yolks, lemon juice, wine, lemon peel, and garlic in food processor. Process, adding oil slowly in a steady stream until well combined. Mix in Parmesan, parsley, salt, and pepper. Adjust seasoning. Pour over cooked asparagus.

Bourbon Walnut Chocolate Pie

This is very similar to today's Derby Pie, which is traditionally served on Derby Day.

Bourbon walnut pie with chunks of chocolate is a decadent dessert.

For the butter crust
2 cups all-purpose flour
2 teaspoons salt
3/4 pound butter
1/2 cup ice water

For the pie
3 large eggs, lightly beaten

1 cup dark Karo corn syrup
1 cup sugar
2 tablespoons melted butter
1 teaspoon vanilla extract
1-1/2 tablespoons bourbon
1-1/2 cups chopped walnuts
2 ounces semisweet chocolate

Put flour, salt, and butter into a mixing bowl and blend with pastry blender or fingers until mixture resembles cornmeal. Add ice water and mix quickly with a fork until dough leaves sides of bowl. Remove dough from bowl and form into a ball. Shape into flat cake and chill for 30 minutes. Roll out to 1/8-inch thickness and put in 9-inch glass pie pan. Flute edges. Combine the first six ingredients in order and mix well. Add walnuts to mixture. Chop chocolate coarsely and place on pie crust. Pour mixture over the chocolate. Bake at 350 degrees for 60 minutes.

Mint Juleps

Traditionally, a mint julep should be served in a special silver julep cup, but any short glass will do fine. Just be sure to top the glass with a bouquet of fresh mint and serve with a straw short enough that the drinker's nose can get buried in the mint.

30 sprigs of mint
24 teaspoons sugar
1/4 cup water
1 liter bourbon whiskey
Crushed ice
Mint for garnish

Remove leaves from the mint. Crush leaves, combine with sugar and water in a saucepan, and bring to a boil. Let stand for at least 1 hour. Chill. Fill each cold glass with crushed ice. Add 1 teaspoon mint syrup and 2 ounces bourbon to each glass. Stir without touching the glass. Garnish with a sprig of mint. Serve immediately.

Mint juleps topped with fresh mint surround an antique cut crystal decanter filled with bourbon.

The Mint Julep

The mint julep is probably the most celebrated and romanticized libation identified with the South. And its origin is truly the plantation. More often than not, the planter's day began with a julep, and in antebellum days, a Southern gentleman may well have rated mixing a mint julep among the fine arts. It has been said that when George Washington took the Marquis de Lafayette to visit his mother in Fredericksburg, she served them mint juleps.

A simple and potent refreshment, the mint julep probably had its beginnings in Virginia. Kentucky, the home of bourbon, lays some claim to its creation, and many give credence to the notion. However, the land that is now Kentucky was still considered the western part of Virginia when it introduced its version of the mint julep.

The formula, secrets, and romantic descriptions of julep making are endless. But it is an uncontested fact that a perfect mint julep must blend two aromas (mint and bourbon) and three flavors (mint, bourbon, and sugar). And none must dominate or overwhelm the others.

The mint julep is a famed part of the races. It is said that one prosperous gentleman, who entertained race enthusiasts profusely each spring, estimated that it took 10,000 mint juleps to get through the weekend.

Summer

The Virginia countryside is a riot of color in early summer. Drifts of confetti-colored blossoms dot the rolling hills. Old-fashioned gardens seem their best in midsummer. Unfurling roses send a delightful fragrance through the air.

Hummingbirds flit about the hollyhocks, foxgloves, and delphiniums. Bright-colored fish move gracefully in the pond. And the sound of moving water encourages a frog to perch upon the lily pads. As warm weather takes hold, thoughts traditionally turn to that most special occasion—a garden wedding. Using nature's bounty of beautiful flowers, fresh herbs, and verdant foliage is a wonderful way to celebrate the joyous events associated with the ritual of marriage. A large patio, an expanse of lawn, or a formal garden beckons a wedding or an outdoor party.

From antebellum days until the early 20th century, a grand lawn party was the traditional way to bring family and friends together on a summer afternoon. Conversation bubbled as games were played and beautifully laid tables were set under the great oak, pine, and maple trees. For a more informal gathering, an old barn, with its steep roof, offers a shady place to set out a barbecue. Hearty and simple, the buffet offers Virginia foods so popular in antebellum days. And a late evening bonfire, marshmallows, and music from a guitar provide a quiet ending to a summer day.

Early summer brought wheat harvesting, the most dramatic of all farm work. Trying to thresh the wheat and beat the summer thunderstorms was a real challenge. It took many hands to bring the wheat up from the fields, load the threshing machines, and stack the straw as it came flying out of the pipe. Two men were delegated just to keep the wildly flowing straw in place. At midday, we set up a table under a big tree to seat the 25 or so men. The meal was a feast. Every pot and pan in the kitchen was pressed into service. Then, everyone went back to work. When all the wheat was harvested on one farm, the threshing machine was moved to the next farm. The men would then follow and continue working into the night. This hectic pace would continue until all the wheat in the area was threshed.

Edna Lewis

A Wedding Dinner

Many brides dream of having a wedding at an old Southern plantation, with its abundance of flowers and nostalgic fragrances of huge boxwood and old roses. They dream of sunlight filtering through the trees and sweet scents wafting from the garden, providing a romantic tranquillity to share with their guests. The plantation provides this classic scenario: acres of rolling grass carpet, a Victorian garden where the mother of the bride can talk with the family, an old-fashioned swing where the bride and groom can be photographed, a veranda from which the bride can throw her bouquet.

The aura of elegance seems to change for each event—expanding, contracting, becoming spacious and then intimate, inviting new ideas and decorations to suit its changing role. One can set off its formality with masses of seasonal flowers from the garden—flowering shrubs, giant peonies, irises. Add a taste of country by using lovely decorations made from daisies, black-eyed Susans, Queen Anne's lace and other flowers growing in the fields. Or make a dramatic statement with an unseasonal choice such as asters or tulips.

The manor house appears to extend into the garden with a great white tent ballooning in the gentle breeze. The tent, with wisteria branches gently cascading from its center poles and baskets overflowing with garden flowers, creates the essential outdoor space. Guests can mingle outside or circulate in the shade it provides. Tables set with a mixture of antique china and silver on damask and lace seem as well placed in the tent as they are in the manor house. Garden-fresh flowers on each table add a further personal touch.

The classic menu is light and festive. Food is arranged without undue fuss, appearing fresh, cool, and colorful. A multi-tiered cake, festooned with fresh flowers, intensifies the nostalgic mood.

When the sun's rays creep across the lawn and late afternoon spills into evening, small lights twinkle on the ceiling of the tent and the glow of candles reflects through the crystal. With the moon above and soft candlelight below, the night seems enchanted.

Green wicker chairs add a festive touch to a country wedding setting.

Willow Grove

Lovely old plantation homes such as this, with their high ceilings, fine floors, and historic appointments, offer a warmth that comes only from having been lived in by generations of families. And Willow Grove was a comfortable house to live in. Although the rooms are large, they are well proportioned, open, and inviting, without the imposing formality so many plantation homes exhibit.

Although in its present incarnation Willow Grove is an inn and restaurant, it still stands as one of the finest examples of Jeffersonian Classical Revival architecture in Orange County. The mansion began as a modest frame house built by Joseph Clark in 1778. In the early

1800s, Clark's son, William, added an imposing brick portion, built by the same craftsmen chosen by Thomas Jefferson to work on the University of Virginia. The original frame dwelling and later brick section are unified by a two-and-one-half story Classical portico with four Tuscan columns. Interestingly, the frame portion retains Federal appointments while Classical Revival appointments dominate the brick addition.

Willow Grove remained in the Clark family for more than 125 years. During that time, William's son, Edwin, married Judith Taliaferro, step-daughter

of James Madison's niece. It was sold in the early 1900s to the Lyne-Shackelford families, who carefully preserved the property.

Today, the structure remains true to its origins. Its original floors, mantels, and woodworking refinements are intact. It is impeccably furnished with a mix of 18th- and 19th-century furnishings. Acres of formal Victorian gardens, huge old boxwoods, and ancient trees dot its landscape. A number of dependent buildings survive from antebellum days, and an early 19th-century frame and stone barn is located beyond.

A Wedding Dinner in the Garden

Menu

Vidalia Onion Bisque

Pecan-Crusted Goat Cheese with Raspberry Vinaigrette

Poached Chesapeake Rockfish with Watercress Mayonnaise

Saffron Risotto Cakes

Baby Green Beans Vinaigrette

Spirited Groom's Cake

Wedding Cake

Lemon Verbena Sorbet

Champagne Punch

Antebellum Wedding Belles

In the antebellum South, marriages were often arranged and, because joining land holdings by marriage increased the wealth of a family, marriage among cousins was common. While children had some freedom in choosing a mate, they were often pressured by their parents with offers of dowries and estates. Thus, a young man commonly asked his father's permission before he asked for the hand of a particular maiden. Parents strictly monitored the courtship, and a gentleman did not propose formally until the fathers of the prospective couple had arranged all necessary financial details.

It's no wonder that proposing was such a traumatic experience for the young man. There was little time for intimacy, and it was accepted that Southern belles were notorious coquettes who often scorned their suitors. Faced with spinsterhood by the age of 20, these young women had a very short time to enjoy the fun and freedom of being a belle before leaving their fathers for husbands.

As a result, belles were fickle and impulsive. And they often played games with their suitors, asking for a second proposal and then refusing or reneging when a more attractive offer came along. But once the engagement was announced, a belle became serious and set about preparing for her wedding, sewing her garb, and assembling her trousseau, often a week's worth of outfits. She knew that, once wed, she would be expected to put aside her capriciousness and settle down to the rigors of running a household.

Like the Old South itself, the antebellum bride epitomized romanticism and sentiment. Her wedding was a joyous occasion that combined old-world traditions with genuine affection and generous hospitality. Often the social event of the season, it was a time of unrestrained merriment.

The ceremony at her home was followed by endless drinking, dancing, and lavish presentations of food. Table after table was filled with vegetables, fruits, meats, cakes, confections, and ices, of which everyone partook while mingling, talking, laughing, and dancing.

A wedding cake festooned with flowers awaits the bride and groom.

Then, well before her guests departed, the bride made a quiet exit to her bedchamber where her mother, sister, and close friends helped her undress and ready her toilette. Then they tucked her into her nuptial bed to receive her groom, who was then tucked in beside her.

Fresh rosemary enhances a bowl of Vidalia onion bisque.

Vidalia Onion Bisque

The flavor of this soup will be greatly different if anything but Vidalia onions are used. Grown only in a special region of Georgia, Vidalia onions have a stronger flavor if grown elsewhere.

3 Vidalia onions
8 tablespoons butter
1/2 cup all-purpose flour
4 cups chicken stock
1 tablespoon kosher salt

1 tablespoon ground pepper
1/2 cup sherry
2 cups heavy cream
3 tablespoons sugar
1/2 cup fresh chives, chopped

Dice onions. Melt butter in a large saucepan. Add onions and sauté until translucent. Add flour and cook over medium heat, stirring constantly for 5 minutes. Add chicken stock and season with salt and pepper. Bring mixture to a boil. Add sherry and cream and simmer for 10 minutes. Add sugar and 1/4 cup of the chives. Remove from heat and pour into bowls. Garnish with remaining chives.

VIDALIA ARE THE SWEETEST ONIONS. I LEARNED ABOUT THEM IN THE 1970S AND LOVED THEM FROM THE FIRST TASTE. THEY MAKE DELICIOUS PICKLES, WHICH ALLOWS YOU TO ENJOY THE SWEET TASTE ALL YEAR LONG. ONE OF MY MOST FAVORITE WAYS TO SERVE THEM IS TO STEAM THEM, CUT OUT THE CENTERS AND FILL THEM WITH FRESH GREEN PEAS. EVERYONE I HAVE MADE THEM FOR AGREES THEY ARE DELICIOUS.

Edna Lewis

The Tussie Mussie

Tussie mussies originated as far back as the Middle Ages when it was thought the fragrance from little bunches of herbs and flowers prevented disease. In the 16th century, ladies began to carry ornamental bouquets to repel offensive odors. Set on a table in a warm room or held in a warm hand, nosegays released pleasant aromas. By the 18th century, the tussie mussie was a popular fashion accessory.

With the 19th century came a passion for flowers. The first English flower book was published. Botany became the theme for wallpapers, carpets, paintings, and other decorating accessories. Ladies learned the Latin name of every flower. The art of botanical printmaking developed. Flower books flooded the market. And the tussie mussie became an essential part of every woman's costume, no matter how simple.

The success of the bouquet depended on the colors and the precision of its arrangement. Usually made of a large flower in the center surrounded by symmetrical rows of flowers and fringed with foliage of evenly distributed colors, the tussie mussie had a lace collar. The stems were wired to thin twigs and wrapped in damp moss. This handle was then wrapped with ribbon or put in a posy holder.

The tussie mussie was part of every young lady's education, as well as wardrobe. Young women were expected to be proficient in floral arts and were taught how to tie beautiful tussie mussies, first at home and then in finishing schools. Detailed directions for making tussie mussies were even published in fashion magazines, and any lady who carried a poorly made bouquet was considered to have poor judgment.

Toward the end of the century, designers were regrouping flowers and concentric circles began to lose favor. When the future Queen Mary married in 1873, she carried an asymmetrical cascade of flowers trailing down to a single flower, an indication of what was to come. By 1890, loose bunches of long-stemmed flowers were in favor, and by the 20th century little was seen of the tussie mussie except for wedding bouquets carried by nostalgic brides.

THE GREAT LITTLE MADISON HAS ASKED . . . TO SEE ME THIS EVENING.
Dolley Madison

A tussie mussie sits beside a traditional tulip vase.

Pecan-Crusted Goat Cheese with Raspberry Vinaigrette

It's a good idea to freeze as many raspberries as you can while they are plentiful. They freeze very well and will keep their flavor for the whole year.

1 12-ounce log goat cheese
1/2 cup pecans, chopped
4 cups baby greens

Roll goat cheese in pecans to coat completely. Wrap tightly in plastic wrap and cut into 1-1/2-inch slices. Serve with greens tossed with raspberry vinaigrette and crackers or melbas.

Raspberry Vinaigrette

1 quart raspberries
1/2 cup red wine vinegar
2 tablespoons sugar
1/2 tablespoon salt
1/2 tablespoon pepper
1/2 small red onion, diced
1/4 cup chopped pecans
2 cups olive oil

Purée raspberries. Combine with vinegar, sugar, salt, and pepper in food processor. Process, adding oil slowly until thoroughly mixed. Add onions and pecans and pulse once or twice to blend.

WE ALWAYS USED WILD RASPBERRIES WHEN WE MADE JAMS AND PRE-SERVES. THEY GROW IN ABUNDANCE IN THE FIELDS AND ON THE EDGES OF WOODLANDS. IF YOU CAN FIND THEM, THEY WOULD BE WONDERFUL IN THIS VINAIGRETTE.

Edna Lewis

Antique Victoria china holds a tempting goat cheese salad.

A Madison Wedding

Not long after the death of Dolley's first husband, and before other suitors could start to call on her, James asked his friend Aaron Burr to set up an introduction. Dolley was so excited that she wrote her friend, Eliza Collins, "Thou must come to me. Aaron Burr says that the great little Madison has asked to be brought out to see me this evening." She then readied for their meeting, donning a mulberry satin dress, matching silk kerchief, and lace cap.

Dolley immediately put James at ease, encouraging the humor that lay beneath the surface of Madison's personality. He fell head over heels in love and within a few months he proposed. But Dolley, not sure this would be the proper step for her so soon after her husband's death, needed some time to make her decision. She set out for Harewood, home of her sister Lucy and husband George Steptoe Washington, nephew of the President. In August, she wrote James that she would marry him and asked him to meet her at Harewood.

Dolley was at Harewood when she received Madison's note of joy. Exuberant, James left Montpelier with his youngest sister, Fanny, and hastened to Harewood. On September 15, 1794, James and Dolley were married in front of the carved green marble mantle in the large Palladian drawing room at Harewood. He wore a silk coat and vest covered with lace ruffles. She wore her engagement ring of rose diamonds, an elaborate necklace and earrings of carved medallions—a wedding present from James.

A garden trellis decorated with an abundance of flowers and greenery makes an unforgettable setting for a wedding ceremony.

The Reverend Alexander Balmain, cousin Lucy Taylor's husband, performed the ceremony. And, although attended only by the immediate family of both Dolley and James, joy and gaiety set the mood. Family lore has it that Fanny Madison and Harriot Washington, along with Dolley, Lucy, and Anna Payne joined in a circle and danced around James that day. Vying with each other for mementos of the celebration, the girls cut pieces of lace from the groom's shirt ruffles.

Still having mixed emotions even on her wedding day, Dolley could not forget that she was leaving the Quaker world of her pious father and deceased husband. Before the ceremony, Dolley wrote to her friend Eliza, who had recently married a non-Quaker congressman. "In the course of this day, I give my Hand to the Man who of all other's I most admire," she wrote. But, after the ceremony, before joining her new husband, Dolley added the postscript, "Evening—Dolley Madison! alass! alass!" Then, amid a shower of rice, she joined her new husband for the ride to Montpelier.

Chesapeake Rockfish with Watercress Mayonnaise

Rockfish is a Virginia delicacy that is only available in late spring and early summer. Any saltwater bass could be substituted in this recipe.

1-1/2 cups chardonnay
4 cups fish stock or bouillon
1 lemon, sliced
3 bay leaves
2 sprigs parsley
6 whole peppercorns
2 shallots, sliced
1 tablespoon salt
4 rockfish fillets

For the mayonnaise
4 egg yolks
1/2 cup fresh lemon juice
4 cups watercress leaves
2 garlic cloves
2 cups olive oil
Cayenne pepper
Freshly ground black pepper
Salt

WATERCRESS GREW WILD NEAR STREAMS ALL AROUND ORANGE COUNTY. THE FLAVOR IS A LOT MORE PEPPERY THAN THAT OF THE WATERCRESS YOU CAN BUY IN THE MARKET. IF IT IS EARLY ENOUGH IN THE SEASON AND YOU CAN FIND IT GROWING WILD, THIS MAYONNAISE WILL BE THE BETTER FOR IT.

Edna Lewis

Combine first 8 ingredients. Bring to a simmer. Do not boil. Add the fish and poach for about 5 minutes or until opaque and flaky. Remove from pan and garnish with lemon and watercress mayonnaise. Combine egg yolks, lemon juice, watercress, and garlic in bowl of food processor. Process, adding oil to egg mixture very slowly and in a steady stream until thickened. Add salt, pepper, and cayenne to taste.

Saffron Risotto Cakes

The creamy texture of the risotto is due to the arborio rice, which can be found in any Italian or specialty market.

2 tablespoons olive oil
1 large onion
2 cups arborio rice
8 cups warm chicken stock
1/2 teaspoon saffron threads

1 cup dry white wine
2 tablespoons butter
1-1/2 cups Romano cheese
Bread crumbs
Salt and pepper

Grate the Romano. Chop the onion and sauté in olive oil until soft and translucent. Add 2 cups arborio rice and sauté briefly, stirring constantly. Add saffron and one cup stock and cook until absorbed, stirring constantly. Add wine and continue cooking until absorbed. Add another cup of stock. As broth is absorbed, continue to add stock, one cup at a time as needed, continuing to stir constantly until rice is *al dente*. Add cheese and butter and mix well. Mixture should be creamy. Season with salt and pepper. Form into cakes about 3 inches in diameter. Dip into bread crumbs. Sauté in butter until lightly browned.

WE OFTEN SERVED GREEN BEENS VINAIGRETTE WITH FRESH TOMATOES. NOT ONLY WAS IT DELICIOUS, IT ALSO LOOKED VERY PRETTY.

Edna Lewis

Green beans vinaigrette look delicious in a Limoges serving dish with gilded handles.

Baby Green Beans Vinaigrette

Select early tender green beans that are slender and about the same length.

1 pound baby green beans
1/2 cup balsamic vinegar
1 cup olive oil
2 teaspoons sugar

Salt and pepper
1/4 cup yellow peppers, diced
1/4 cup red peppers, diced
1/4 cup red onion, diced

Blanch green beans in boiling water until just tender. Combine balsamic vinegar, olive oil, and sugar. Whisk together until blended. Season with salt and pepper to taste. Add baby green beans, yellow and red peppers, and onion. Toss to cover well.

Spirited Groom's Cake

An updated rendition of a very old Pennsylvania recipe, this delicious cake is dark and moist without being overly sweet.

2 cups sugar	2 eggs
2 cups all-purpose flour	1 cup milk
2 teaspoons baking powder	1 teaspoon vanilla
1 teaspoon baking soda	1/4 cup bourbon
3/4 cup cocoa	3/4 cup boiling coffee
1/2 cup vegetable oil	

Preheat oven to 375 degrees. Grease and flour two 9-inch layer cake pans. Sift together sugar, flour, baking powder, baking soda, and cocoa. Add oil, eggs, milk, and vanilla. Beat well. Add bourbon to boiling coffee. Add to batter and mix well with a spoon. Mixture will be very thin. Pour into cake pans. Bake 25 minutes.

Chocolate Bourbon Icing

A nice alternative to this icing is bourbon-flavored whipped cream.

1 egg, beaten	1/4 cup butter
3 tablespoons bourbon	2 ounces unsweetened
1 teaspoon lemon juice	chocolate
1 teaspoon vanilla extract	2-1/2 cups confectioner's sugar

Combine egg, bourbon, lemon juice, and vanilla in small mixing bowl. Stir until well blended. Set aside. Cream butter in medium mixing bowl. Melt chocolate, add to butter, and beat until smooth. Gradually add sugar to mixture alternately with bourbon mixture. Beat until smooth.

Sugar Cake Figurines

The wedding cake figurines popular in the 19th and early 20th centuries were descendants of sugar allegories made by 18th-century confectioners. These scenes, which usually consisted of a sugar temple surrounded by sugar gods, were made in several different ways: by running sugar syrup around the inside of an alabaster mold to form a hollow figure; by mixing sugar, gum tragacanth, and coloring together and pressing into a mold; or by modeling the sugar-gum mixture by hand.

People discovered that the edible figures made pretty decorations on cakes for gala occasions. Cakes made for Twelfth Night feasts were traditionally covered with a hard white icing and crowned with one more of these sugar-and-gum figures.

Three-dimensional sugar birds, cherubs, fruit, castles, and other images soon made their way as ornaments on the top of cakes to celebrate birthdays, anniversaries, and graduations. Not surprisingly, little brides and grooms, some with doves and other ornaments, were soon adorning wedding cakes throughout the South.

Lemon Verbena Sorbet

Virginia gardens were known to have an abundance of herbs as early as the 18th century.

2 cups sugar
3 to 4 cups lemon verbena leaves
5 cups water

Chop verbena leaves. Combine with sugar and water and place in saucepan. Bring to boil. Reduce heat to low and simmer 5 minutes. Let cool. Chill at least 8 hours. Strain. Freeze according to instructions on ice cream freezer.

An heirloom silver punch bowl is waiting for champagne.

OUR HEARTS UNDER-STAND EACH OTHER.

Dolley Madison

Champagne Punch

Allow plenty of time for the ice to freeze before you plan to serve this punch.

For fruited ice block
1 quart water
1 cup sliced fruit

For the punch
1 quart fresh lemonade
1 fifth gin
2 quarts ginger ale
2 fifths champagne

Wash and fill a half-gallon paper milk container with water. Add sliced fruit and put in freezer. Freeze until firm, shaking occasionally to distribute fruit throughout. Combine first two ingredients in large punch bowl. Remove carton from fruited ice block and place in bowl. Add ginger ale and champagne. Serve immediately.

A Fourth of July Barbecue

Wild grasses ring the pond while daisies, black-eyed Susans, and purple coneflowers fill the fields. Crickets chirp in new-mown hay and butterflies hang almost motionless over the Queen Anne's lace.

Recalling antebellum days, the plantation celebrates the Fourth of July with an old-fashioned barbecue, much as it would have been in the 18th century. Tablecloths, dishes, and napery in red, white, and blue sound a patriotic note. An heirloom red pitcher holds an arrangement of wild grasses. Homespun linens and old rag rugs provide a charming country look.

A weathered country table covered with an antique red-and-white quilt and heaped with family favorites forms the heart of a country meal. Cobalt blue Fiesta ware pitchers hold wildflowers from the meadow. Rustic holders for red and blue napkins complement the table arrangements.

An antique red and white quilt complements the red, white, and blue of the dishes.

A mixture of heirloom Fiesta ware, Mary Hadley Pottery, Stangle, and Spatterware displays hearty and typically Southern food: a pit-roasted pig dripping in its juices, platters of barbecued baby back ribs, Virginia fried chicken, tender grilled zucchini and eggplant brushed with olive oil and garlic, a streusel pie of just-picked peaches, and

sweet biscuit cobbler topped with fresh homemade ice cream.

Fresh-roasted Virginia peanuts, along with kegs of cold beer and pitchers of old-time lemonade, help stave off hunger while the pig cooks. Horseshoes, badminton, and volleyball keep everyone entertained once they have feasted.

Somerset

Somerset Plantation sits majestically on a hill overlooking the Virginia countryside. A winding driveway leads to this well-preserved structure.

The mansion, which is located across Blue Run from Montpelier, was built in 1803 by Sarah Madison, sister of the President, and her husband, Thomas Macon. The Macons were neighbors of James and Dolley for nearly 50 years. They seem to have been occupied with farming, social activities, and their family. Their children and grandchildren had a warm and close relationship with James and Dolley and often visited each other.

A Federal style brick mansion, the house has two

stories over an English basement and a hipped roof. Both of the two rooms that flank each side of a central hallway have interior chimneys. An elaborate archway separates this central hallway from a smaller hallway behind. Like many of the Jeffersonian-style homes in Orange, there is no grand staircase. Rather, a modest enclosed stairway rises from one of the rooms.

The elaborate Federal woodworking on mantels, cornices, archways, and wainscoting remains. The porches, however, were added much later.

A Fourth of July Barbecue

Menu

Roasted Suckling Pig

Barbecued Baby Back Ribs

Virginia Fried Chicken

Potato Salad with Herbs

Wilted Greens with Warm Bacon Dressing

Grilled Zucchini and Eggplant

Fresh Corn Hush Puppies

Blackberry Cobbler

Hand-Churned Honey Vanilla Ice Cream

Old-Time Lemonade

Madison Barbecues

James Madison's retirement brought everyone—family, friends, heads of state, foreign dignitaries, famous authors—to Montpelier. The Madisons shared their table, offered a bed, and provided conversation and entertainment to everyone alike. Many often joined the Madison family and friends at Dolley's grand back lawn feasts that Dolley spread under the tall oaks. The grounds were alive with carriages, horses, servants, and children. Appetites were whetted by the invigorating mountain air.

Very often a simple barbecue, these get-togethers were very different from Dolley's elegant Washington soirees. Nonetheless, Dolley's visitors were tantalized with the lavish display of food and hospitality. Whole pigs roasted on the spit and tables groaned under the sumptuous spread while farmers exchanged ideas about both crops and politics. If it was not too late, slaves entertained with fiddle playing, singing, and dancing while wine and conversation flowed freely.

On more special occasions, field hands often were summoned from their usual tasks to help with party preparations. They offered trays laden with food as the guests joined in lively conversation and local gossip. At the end of the evening, they often served as chambermaids to aid those remaining overnight. Then they retired, feasting off the remains of the repast and making the night melodious with their songs.

WHERE WILL YOU CELEBRATE THE FOURTH OF JULY, MY DEAR SISTER? WE ARE TO HAVE GRAND DOINGS HERE.

Dolley Madison

A suckling pig surrounded with fruits is a favorite Fourth of July picnic fare.

Pit Roasting

Pit roasting came into Southern cooking early in our history. Native Americans were roasting meat over open fires when the colonists settled in Virginia during the 1600s. By the early 1800s, the smoky, pit-roasted and sauce-doused pig was a Southern favorite, and pit barbecues had become the primary form of summer entertainment on the plantation. Although the practice was not confined to the plantation, it took root there because of the pool of labor available to do the hot, difficult work of digging, lugging, and turning the spit. But regardless of the work, no other food on the plantation was regarded with more enthusiasm than a perfectly cooked and seasoned pit-cooked pig.

Roasting a pig in antebellum days was an all-night ritual. It began in early evening when a crew of strong-arms dug a huge pit, lined it with rocks and set a blazing fire of applewood logs and grapevines. Hours later, when the pit was glowing, the crew put the pigs on spits and suspended them on racks above the coals. There they spent the night stoking the fire as the pig cooked to a tenderness that is hard to imagine. As the fragrance of smoldering wood mingled with the aroma of slowly roasting pork, the fire tenders spun long tales until morning.

While the custom continues today, it is more likely that a small suckling pig or pork shoulder would replace the hogs of antebellum days and the oven or grill would replace the pit.

Roasted Suckling Pig

The pig can also be cooked the entire time in the oven at 325 degrees for about 3-1/2 hours.

1 18- to 20-pound suckling pig
Kosher salt
Cracked peppercorns
Fresh thyme and edible flowers
1 whole red apple

Preheat oven to 325 degrees. Rub cavity of the pig with the salt and pepper. Stuff the cavity with aluminum foil to help pig keep its shape during roasting. Set pig on its stomach in roasting pan. Curl feet under its body. Open its mouth and put in a block of wood or small ball of foil. Roast for about 2-1/2 hours. Remove pig from oven and cool slightly. Remove foil from cavity and put pig on spit. Place spit on grill over hot coals. Cook for an additional 45 minutes, or until the skin is evenly brown and clear juices run when it is pricked with a fork. Remove pig from grill and place on large serving board. Remove spit from pig. Place an apple in the pig's mouth and surround its neck with fresh thyme and edible flowers.

WE OFTEN STUFFED OUR PIG WITH A COMBINATION OF PORK LIVER, LEAN PORK, CHICKEN LIVERS, CHESTNUTS, AND PEACHES SEASONED WITH A LOT OF HERBS AND SPICES. IT WAS DELICIOUS.

Edna Lewis

Baby Back Ribs

Boiling the ribs makes them tender, reduces the fat, and results in a shorter grilling time.

5 pounds baby back ribs
Worcestershire sauce
Salt and pepper

Fill a stock pot 2/3 full of water. Add Worcestershire, salt, and pepper to season water. Bring to a boil. Add ribs and cook for 30-40 minutes or until the meat of the ribs is breaking off the bones. Remove the ribs and let cool. Grill ribs, basting occasionally with barbecue sauce.

No barbecue is complete without good fresh bread and an array of just-picked summer vegetables.

Barbecue Sauce

Many good barbecue sauces can be found in the supermarket, but there is something special about serving a homemade sauce.

2 cups tomato sauce
1 cup catsup
1 tablespoon spicy mustard
1/4 cup red wine vinegar
2 tablespoons Worcestershire
2 tablespoons clarified butter
3 tablespoons brown sugar
1 teaspoon cayenne

2 tablespoons paprika
2 tablespoons chili powder
1 teaspoon red pepper
1 teaspoon dry mustard
2 tablespoons honey
1 tablespoon molasses
Salt and pepper

WE HAD NINETY PERSONS TO DINE WITH US AT ONE TABLE–PUT UP ON THE LAWN, UNDER A THICK ARBOR.

Dolley Madison

Combine ingredients in a saucepan. Bring to boil and simmer for about 5 minutes. Correct seasoning. Let cool and refrigerate. Use as a marinade or basting for barbecued chicken, ribs, or pulled pork.

Virginia Fried Chicken

This is the fried chicken that Edna Lewis taught us to make on her many trips to Willow Grove. Soaking the chicken in cold buttermilk and letting it rest after it is coated are her secrets for the best chicken.

2 2-pound frying chickens, cut into 8 pieces each
1 quart water
1 tablespoon salt
1 quart cold buttermilk

1 cup all-purpose flour
1 cup whole wheat flour
1/2 cup lard or shortening
1/2 cup butter
1 teaspoon fresh pepper

Cover the chicken pieces with salt water and set aside in refrigerator overnight. Remove from water, dry thoroughly and cover with buttermilk. Set aside in refrigerator overnight. Combine the flours with the salt and pepper. Mix well. Drain buttermilk from the chicken and dry lightly with a damp cloth. Roll each piece of chicken in the flour mixture and set aside for an hour. Put the lard or shortening in a skillet and heat until smoking. Add the butter. When the butter is melted, add the chicken. Turn heat to high, cover the pan, and brown the chicken about 10-12 minutes on each side, turning frequently to assure even browning.

*M*Y MOTHER ALWAYS MADE A NICE BROWN CREAM GRAVY FOR THIS CHICKEN BY ADDING FLOUR TO SOME OF THE RESERVED FAT, QUICKLY BROWNING IT, AND THEN ADDING FRESH SWEET CREAM, WHICH WAS ALWAYS PLENTIFUL IN THE SUMMER ONCE THE CALVES WERE WEANED.

Edna Lewis

Potato Salad with Herbs

Any potato can be used in this recipe, but it is especially delicious with early summer potatoes that recently have been dug from the garden.

2 pounds new potatoes
1 tablespoon Dijon mustard
2 cups red onion, chopped
1/2 cup parsley, chopped
1 teaspoon dill, chopped

1-1/2 teaspoons chopped thyme
1/2 teaspoon celery seed
1/2 teaspoon salt
1 teaspoon coarse black pepper
3/4 cup mayonnaise

Wash and scrub potatoes, but do not peel. Cook in a large pot of boiling water until soft but still firm. Drain and cool. Cut into 3/4-inch pieces. Toss with Dijon mustard to coat well. Add onions, parsley, dill, thyme, celery seed, salt, pepper, and mayonnaise and blend lightly.

Wilted Greens with Warm Bacon Dressing

Greens with a warm bacon dressing were served at Southern tables as early as the Revolutionary War. Dandelions, lettuce, spinach, endive, and cabbage all can be used, depending on the season.

2 egg yolks
1/4 cup fresh lemon juice
1 garlic clove
1 cup olive oil
Salt

Freshly ground black pepper
Cayenne pepper
8 cups mixed greens
6 slices applewood-smoked
    bacon

Combine egg yolks, lemon juice, and garlic in bowl of food processor. Process, adding oil to egg mixture very slowly and in a steady stream until mixture is thickened. Add salt, pepper, and cayenne to taste. Refrigerate. Just before serving, wash greens and tear into medium-sized pieces. Dry greens completely and put in bowl. Cook bacon over medium heat until crisp. Remove bacon and drain on paper towels. Pour warm bacon drippings over greens and toss lightly to wilt. Add refrigerated dressing a tablespoon at a time, tossing lightly. Crumble bacon on top and serve immediately.

*W*E HAD WILTED LETTUCE WHEN THERE WASN'T MUCH ELSE IN THE GARDEN—AT THE END OF SPRING AND BEFORE THE SUMMER VEGETABLES WERE READY.

Edna Lewis

Grilled Zucchini and Eggplant

Purple eggplant was popular with the colonists, but we prefer to use the white variety since it is much less bitter. Baby eggplant and zucchini found in early summer are especially delicious.

1 cup olive oil
2 cloves garlic, minced
2 tablespoons chopped herbs

3 eggplants
5 zucchini
Salt and pepper

Peel and slice eggplants. Slice zucchini. Combine oil, garlic, and herbs. Season to taste with salt and pepper. Marinate vegetables for at least 2 hours. Grill over hot coals for about 2 minutes on each side.

Fresh Corn Hush Puppies

The true origin of hush puppies is not known, but it is believed they were created as an accompaniment to freshly caught and fried fish.

2 ears fresh corn
1 cup cornmeal
2/3 cup flour
3 teaspoons baking powder
1 teaspoon baking soda

3 tablespoons sugar
1 teaspoon salt
1/2 onion, diced
1 cup buttermilk
Oil for deep frying

Husk and wash corn. Sift together dry ingredients. Cut kernels from cob. Mix with onion and dry ingredients. Add buttermilk and mix just until moistened. Refrigerate for at least 2 hours. Place oil in deep skillet and heat to 350 degrees. Drop mixture into hot oil by the tablespoonful. Fry until golden brown and dry in the center.

Corn is most tender and sweet when cooked as soon as it has been picked from the field.

Hominy Grits

Corn is the ultimate American grain. For hundreds of years before the Europeans reached the shores of North America, Indians were drying hulled corn into hominy. They stewed whole hominy with meat and field greens, crushed it and mixed it with fish to make a soup, ground it into grits which they served with salt pork and maple syrup, and pounded it into a meal from which they made suppone, a type of bread.

Shortly after they landed at Jamestown, Virginia, the settlers learned creative ways to apply Indian methods of cooking this grain. And they soon realized the benefit of adding cornmeal to flour when making bread. One recipe followed another, and various refinements developed. This evolution of cornbread from suppone to the types we enjoy today parallels the social and cultural traditions and history of the South.

In colonial and antebellum days, cornbreads were eaten throughout the Southern plantation region as though no other bread existed. All the pone-type breads were widely known—from primitive ashcake to hoecake to corn pones to johnnycake. Crispy morsels of rendered fat called cracklings, a by-product of hog killing on the plantation, soon found their way into the pone.

Cornbread dressing, griddle cakes, muffins, and cornsticks were later refinements of baked cornbread. Hush puppies, cakes fried in hot oil and eaten either hot or cold, soon followed. Often taken on fishing trips, hush puppies got their name from fishermen who threw the cakes to the dogs to keep them quiet.

The ultimate use for cornmeal came with the development of spoonbread, a feather-light dish of cornmeal mixed with butter, eggs, milk, and seasonings for which the South is famous.

Blackberry Cobbler

BLACKBERRIES GREW IN ABUNDANCE DURING THE EARLY SUMMER AND WERE RIPE JUST IN TIME FOR WHEAT THRESHING. WE WOULD GO BLACKBERRY PICKING EARLY IN THE MORNING AND COLLECT A QUART OR GALLON IN NO TIME. WE THEN LOOKED FORWARD TO MOTHER MAKING A COBBLER TO SERVE AT DINNER.

Edna Lewis

As in Colonial days, Virginia blackberries are ripe just in time for the Fourth of July, and they make a wonderful cobbler for a cookout.

For the cobbler
4 cups fresh blackberries
2 tablespoons flour
1/2 teaspoon cinnamon
1/2 cup sugar

For the biscuit crust
1 cup flour
1/4 teaspoon salt
1 tablespoon sugar
1/2 teaspoon baking powder
3 tablespoons butter
6 tablespoons light cream

Preheat oven to 425 degrees. Gently toss together blackberries, flour, cinnamon, and sugar. Set aside. Mix together flour, salt, sugar, and baking powder. Cut in butter. Add cream and stir with fork until mixture leaves sides of bowl. Knead lightly, about 10 times, until mixture is smooth and not sticky. Roll out to 10-inch square. Pour fruit mixture into greased 9-inch baking dish. Top with rolled-out crust. Sprinkle lightly with sugar. Bake for 35 minutes.

Freshly baked blackberry cobbler is a favorite Virginia ending to a summer meal.

Much of the fun of a summer picnic is joining friends and family together to churn the ice cream.

I LIKE TO ADD ABOUT A TEASPOON OR SO OF SALT TO THE ICE CREAM MIX. THE SALT REALLY BRINGS OUT THE FLAVOR, ESPE- CIALLY IN VANILLA. TRY IT AND EXPERIMENT WITH THE QUANTITY YOURSELF.

Edna Lewis

Hand-Churned Honey Vanilla Ice Cream

We prefer to use the old-fashioned wooden ice cream freezer. It takes more work, but it can provide a fun time for family or guests. Just be sure the dasher is very cold.

10 ounces honey
1 quart half-and-half
18 egg yolks, slightly beaten

2 cups sugar
1 quart heavy cream
Vanilla extract

Scald half-and-half. Add honey and stir well. Beat egg yolks and sugar to- gether. Slowly add half-and-half mixture to egg yolk mixture. Transfer to clean saucepan and make a custard. Cool custard in ice bath. Add 1 quart heavy cream. Add vanilla to taste. Chill ingredients. Freeze according to directions on ice cream freezer.

Fiesta, spatterware, and Mary Hadley pottery combine to make an interesting buffet table.

Old-Time Lemonade

Cooking the lemon rind gives this lemonade a hearty lemon flavor.

6 large lemons
2 cups sugar
6 cups water

Wash lemons and roll on a flat surface to soften. Remove outer rinds and cut into strips. Set aside. Combine sugar and water in a medium saucepan. Bring to a boil. Add lemon strips. Cover and simmer about 5 minutes or until thickened. Remove from heat and discard rind. Cool. Squeeze lemons and strain juice. Add to syrup to make a base. Add water until desired strength is reached.

An Afternoon Lawn Party

Informal parties are a wonderful way to spend a summer day or evening. As sunlight filters through the branches of ancient trees, the plantation is the perfect backdrop for an old-fashioned lawn party.

Small tables surround a large buffet table and a bar from which drinks are served. Tables are set with an assortment of old Blue Ridge Pottery. Antique wicker chairs surround each table. Bright garden flowers in old baskets complement the Blue Ridge colors, resulting in a coordinated summery and refreshing look.

The menu reflects the best of the season, with a bounty of fruits and vegetables from the garden or the farmer's market—freshly picked ears of sweet corn, red ripe tomatoes, crisp cucumbers, juicy peaches. Searching for superb quality and just-picked freshness is entertainment in itself. And, to top off the day, nothing could be more perfect than hand-churned ice cream and a game of croquet.

A centerpiece of wild flowers complements antique wicker chairs at a summer luncheon.

Woodberry Forest

Woodberry Forest is a 200-year-old landmark whose history blends the heritage of the Madison family with that of Thomas Jefferson. A grove of stately trees, some as old as the house, shade the entire front of the mansion.

The house was built in 1793 by William Madison, brother of the President.

few miles from Montpelier, and fathered ten children. This may have distracted him from law for a while, although he did serve two terms in the Virginia legislature.

Woodberry Forest was constructed as a modest seven-room Palladian-style house according to a floor plan suggested by Jefferson.

porch on each end of the house, an octagonal room at the rear, bow windows on the front, dormers in the steep roof, and a dining room in the east basement.

Now the Headmaster's residence at Woodberry Forest, a prominent boys' school, the house has been renamed The Residence. It boasts a Sheraton sideboard that was originally in the William Madison dining room.

William was much younger than James and therefore not a companion in his early years. Nor was he as close to James as his other siblings during their adult years. He was, however, mentioned among the guests at Montpelier and did share his brother's political views. He studied law for a time under Jefferson. But he married, built Woodberry Forest on a farm a

Jefferson's design influence is visible in the floor plan and single-story height, the Palladian portico with Tuscan columns resting on a soapstone porch, the high basement, and some of the interior woodwork.

The property passed from the Madison family to the Walker family in 1872. The Walkers added a wing, an open

This Sheraton sideboard belonged to William Madison.

An Afternoon Lawn Party

Menu

Chilled Leek and Potato Bisque

Baby Greens with Virginia Peanut Vinaigrette

Chesapeake Crab Cakes

Smoked Game Hens

Peach and Pecan Chutney

Silver Queen Corn Pudding

Sweet Potato Cobbler

Scalloped Tomatoes

Wilted Sweet-and-Sour Cucumbers

Streusel Peach Pie

Almond Macaroons

Fresh French Vanilla Ice Cream

Minted Iced Tea

Antebellum Pastimes

The rural and agrarian nature of the antebellum plantation had much to do with shaping the diversions of the planter and his family. Since the plantation was completely self-sustaining and had little or no need for marketplaces, town centers such as those developing in the North were virtually nonexistent.

Without these centers to provide activity and camaraderie, Southerners looked to their families and close friends for social pastimes. Ladies amused themselves primarily by visiting each other, often to spend the day quilting, sewing, and gardening together.

Anxious to enliven her lonely existence, and lacking the elaborate restaurants, theaters, and operas of the larger, more populated Northern cities, the plantation mistress always stood ready to receive guests, with or without an invitation, and to hostess any type of social activity—a hunt, dinner, picnic, or party.

Hosting a party on the lawn was an especially popular way to entertain. A sunny summer Sunday afternoon offered her the perfect excuse to set out an opulent affair, complete with drinks, lively conversation, and a magnificent feast set out under the trees.

The day often started early and went on into the night since most guests had traveled a considerable distance and would likely stay the night. The party had particular emphasis on gaming. Lawn tennis, horseshoes, badminton, and croquet were played before and after the luncheon. Cards, chess, and dice entertained the gentlemen when the sun went down.

All in all, this friendly gathering stimulated an environment of hospitality that far surpassed anything known in the North.

Hand-painted flowers on Blue Ridge pottery add a summery note to a lawn party.

Chilled Leek and Potato Bisque

Leeks are very sandy, so be sure to wash them well.

1 stick unsalted butter
3 large leeks, chopped
3 large potatoes, chopped
8 cups chicken stock
3 cups cold milk
2 cups cold heavy cream
2/3 cup chopped chives
salt and pepper

Melt butter to foaming stage. Add leeks and potatoes and mix well. Cover and place over medium heat for about 15 minutes. This will allow the flavors of the leeks and potatoes to meld. Be careful that they don't stick or burn. Add chicken stock and cook for about an hour. Cool mixture. Add salt and pepper to potato-leek mixture and purée in blender. Chill. Add the milk and cream. Keep chilled until serving time. Garnish with the chopped chives.

I LIKE TO COOK THE LEEKS AND POTATOES WITHOUT ADDING ANY WATER. IT GIVES THE SOUP A REAL GOOD FLAVOR AND SENDS WONDERFUL AROMAS THROUGHOUT THE KITCHEN.

Edna Lewis

Baby Greens with Virginia Peanut Vinaigrette

This recipe makes about 6 pints of dressing. It will keep a long time if kept covered in the refrigerator.

For Creole seasoning
3/4 teaspoon paprika
1/2 teaspoon salt
1/2 teaspoon garlic powder
1/4 teaspoon black pepper
1/4 teaspoon onion powder
1/4 teaspoon cayenne pepper
1/4 teaspoon oregano
1/4 teaspoon thyme

For the vinaigrette
4 shallots, quartered

3-1/2 cups salted peanuts
2 ounces molasses
4 teaspoons brown sugar
2 teaspoons salt
1 teaspoon black pepper
1/4 cup balsamic vinegar
3 cups white wine vinegar
1/2 cup red wine vinegar
3 dashes Tabasco sauce
2 dashes Worcestershire sauce
1 teaspoon peanut butter
1 quart canola oil

Mix spices together for Creole seasoning. Set aside. Mix all ingredients for vinaigrette together. Add 2 tablespoons Creole seasoning. Blend to emulsify. Toss over baby greens.

Chesapeake Crab Cakes

The Chesapeake Bay provides some of the finest crabs in the country, and there is nothing better in the summer than these succulent crab cakes. Buy the freshest crab you can find and be sure to pick out all the little bits of shell that are always present in the meat.

OTHER THAN THE OYSTERS THAT APPEARED AT CHRISTMASTIME IN ORANGE, WE NEVER HAD ANY FISH THAT WASN'T CAUGHT IN NEARBY LAKES AND STREAMS. WHEN I WORKED IN CHARLESTON, THOUGH, I FELL IN LOVE WITH CRAB. I CAN NOW TRULY SAY THAT I DON'T KNOW OF ONE CRAB DISH I DON'T LOVE.

Edna Lewis

2 pounds jumbo lump crab
8 slices white bread
4 tablespoons butter
1/2 cup scallions
1 cup heavy cream
Several dashes Tabasco sauce
Salt and pepper
8 lemon wedges

Pick crab, being careful not to break up the lumps, to remove all bits of shell. Set aside. Trim crusts off bread and pulse in food processor until soft crumbs are formed. Toss bread crumbs in crab meat to soak up the moisture. Sauté scallions in the butter until slightly soft. Mix cream and Tabasco and add scallions and butter to mixture. Add cream mixture to crab, a little at a time until crab mixture holds together. Season to taste with salt and pepper. Shape into cakes and sauté in butter about 3 minutes on each side until golden brown. Garnish with lemon wedges.

There is nothing tastier than succulent Chesapeake crab cakes.

Smoked Game Hens

We have found that there are butchers who sell hens that are already smoked. You need only to finish them in a hot oven.

8 small game hens
1 gallon water
8 cloves garlic, smashed
3/4 cup salt
1/4 cup sugar

1/4 cup sage
1/4 cup chili powder
1/2 cup jerk seasoning
1/4 cup cumin
1 teaspoon black pepper

Cover wood chips with water and let soak for 24 hours. Combine water, garlic, and spices to make a brine. Put hens in brine and soak over night. Remove hens from liquid and drain. Place charcoal in a smoker, light coals, and allow to burn until mostly gray. Fill water pan in smoker with water to help keep hens moist. Moderate temperature. Spray grill with vegetable spray. Shake water off wood chips and add to hot coals. Place hens on grill inside smoker. Close lid and let smoke for 1 to 2 hours. Add more chips as necessary. Before serving, put in 160-degree oven for 15-20 minutes to finish cooking and heat through.

*T*OMORROW I EXPECT A LARGE PARTY FROM RICH-MOND AND THE LOWER COUNTRY TO STAY WITH US.

Dolley Madison

Peach and Pecan Chutney

This chutney is a good way to preserve peaches for the rest of the year.

10 ripe peaches
1 small onion
1 cup raisins
1 cup pecan halves
1 cup brown sugar

1 cup white vinegar
1 teaspoon nutmeg
1 teaspoon cinnamon
1 teaspoon ginger

Peel and dice peaches. Dice onion and chop pecans. Combine all ingredients except the pecans. Place in a saucepan and bring to a boil. Simmer for about 10 minutes or until thickened to a pulp. Add pecans and remove from heat.

Silver Queen Corn Pudding

When cutting corn from the cob, it is very important to cut through only half of the kernel and then scrape the rest of the corn off the cob with a butter knife.

1 dozen ears fresh corn	2 cups half-and-half
1/3 cup sugar	3 tablespoons melted butter
1 teaspoon salt	1/2 teaspoon fresh nutmeg
2 eggs, beaten	

Preheat oven to 350 degrees. Cut enough corn from the cob to make 2 cups. Add sugar and salt and stir well. Mix eggs together with the half-and-half and pour over corn mixture. Mix thoroughly and spoon into a well- buttered casserole. Sprinkle top with nutmeg. Set casserole in a pan of hot water and bake for about 35 minutes until set.

*N*OTHING IN THE SUMMER BEATS FRESH CORN ON THE COB. WHEN I WAS GROWING UP, WE COULDN'T GET ENOUGH OF IT. I RE-MEMBER HAVING CORN AND TOMATOES FOR LUNCH AND THEN HAVING CORN AGAIN AS A SEPARATE COURSE AT DINNER. UNLIKE THE SWEET CORN WE KNOW TODAY, THE FIELD CORN WE HAD WAS VERY MEATY, AND WE SOME-TIMES BAKED IT IN THE HUSK, WHICH MADE IT A LITTLE CRISP. NOW WHEN I BOIL IT, I OFTEN LEAVE IT IN THE HUSK TO KEEP THE MOISTURE IN.

Edna Lewis

Sweet Potato Cobbler

This is a twist on the sweet potato pie served at summer gatherings throughout Virginia and the South.

For the pastry	1/2 cup sugar
1-1/4 cups flour	1/4 teaspoon each cinna-
1 cup chilled butter	mon, nutmeg, and salt
Dash of salt	2 eggs
1/2 cup cold water	1 teaspoon vanilla extract
	1/2 cup melted butter
For the filling	1-1/2 cups half-and-half
1 cup cooked sweet potatoes	

With a pastry blender, mix flour, butter, and salt to the consis-tency of coarse meal. Add cold water and mix together until mixture leaves the sides of the bowl. Remove from bowl, shape into a ball, and chill in refrigerator. Put sweet potatoes through a sieve and combine with sugar, spices, eggs, vanilla, and butter. Mix thoroughly and stir in the half-and-half. Pour batter into buttered pie pan. Roll out pastry to 1/8-inch thickness and place over the batter. Pierce dough to allow air to escape as it bakes. Bake at 350 degrees for about 45 minutes or until pastry is golden brown.

Scalloped Tomatoes

As popular as tomatoes are in the summer today, it is hard to believe they were once thought to be poisonous. Before 1850, they were known as "love apples" and planted only in flower gardens.

5 pounds ripe tomatoes
3 slices cubed bread
1/2 cup water

4 tablespoons sugar
6 tablespoons butter
Salt and pepper

Preheat oven to 375 degrees. Drop tomatoes into very hot water and let sit for a minute or two. Remove tomatoes. When cool enough to handle, peel off skins. Quarter them and remove as many seeds as possible. Place in a saucepan with the water and cook for about 15 minutes. Add sugar and salt and pepper. Butter a casserole and line bottom with bread cubes. Top bread crumbs with a layer of tomatoes. Dot with butter. Continue layering bread cubes and tomatoes, ending with the bread. Dot top with the last of the butter. Bake for about 35 minutes.

Scalloped tomatoes in a tulip bowl are pretty as well as tasty.

Wilted Sweet-and-Sour Cucumbers

This sweet-and-sour dressing provides a different way to prepare the ever-plentiful summer cucumbers.

4 cucumbers
Salt
4 slices applewood-smoked
  bacon

1 tablespoon sugar
Cracked pepper
1 tablespoon cider vinegar

Peel cucumbers and slice paper thin. Spread slices on large platter, sprinkle with salt and let stand for half an hour. Dice bacon and fry slowly until crisp and brown. Drain on paper towels until all grease is removed. Drain cucumbers well and mix with bacon. Sprinkle with sugar and pepper. Add vinegar. Cover pan and simmer gently for 20 minutes. Sprinkle with crumbled bacon.

*D*URING HARVEST SEASON, WE ALWAYS HAD TOMATOES THICKENED WITH BREAD AND BAKED WITH LOTS OF BUTTER AND SUGAR. THEY ADDED A FESTIVE TOUCH TO OUR MEALS.

Edna Lewis

The crunch of the streusel and the slight tartness of the peaches provide a nice contrast to the smooth, sweet ice cream.

Croquet

Croquet was played by kings in France as early as the 16th century. In the 18th century, it was played by royalty and upper-class Englishmen who called it "crookery" after the shepherds' crooks used for clubs.

The game, which came to America in the 1870s, is played by using a croquet mallet to roll a one-pound ball consecutively through six cast-iron hoops that are barely large enough for the ball to pass through. Originally played in England on an 84- by 105-foot green, croquet was perfectly suited to the wide lawns of Southern estates.

Throughout Victorian times, croquet and other sports played on the green remained popular. Parties were held before and after the games. And the luncheon that accompanied croquet was as expansive as the estate on which the game was played. For any old-fashioned summer lawn party, croquet is a must.

Almond Macaroons

Almond macaroons have been baked in America since Colonial days and were one of Thomas Jefferson's favorite desserts. We like to think Dolley served them to him when he visited Montpelier.

8 ounces chopped almonds
6 tablespoons soft butter
1 cup powdered sugar

1 cup all-purpose flour
1 teaspoon almond extract
6 egg whites

Preheat oven to 325 degrees. Lay almonds out on a cookie sheet in a single layer and toast until lightly browned, about 3-5 minutes. Remove from oven and let cool. Using an electric mixer, cream butter, sugar, flour, and almond extract into a paste. Incorporate egg whites quickly, beating on medium speed. Fold in toasted almonds. Line cookie sheet with wax paper or coat with vegetable spray. Scoop batter onto cookie sheet with small scoop or teaspoon. Bake for 10-15 minutes, or until golden brown.

Streusel Peach Pie

For the butter crust
2 cups all-purpose flour
2 teaspoons salt
3/4 pound butter
1/2 cup ice water

For the filling
10 fresh peaches
1 cup sour cream
1 cup sugar

1 teaspoon cinnamon
1 egg, beaten
3 tablespoons flour
1 tablespoon vanilla

For the topping
1 cup sugar
1-1/2 cups flour
1 tablespoon cinnamon
1 cup cold butter

Preheat oven to 375 degrees. Put flour, salt, and butter into a mixing bowl of food processor and pulse until mixture resembles cornmeal. Add ice water and mix quickly with a fork until dough leaves the sides of the bowl. Remove from bowl and shape into a flat cake. Chill for 30 minutes. Roll out to 1/8-inch thickness and put into a 9-inch glass pie pan. Flute edges and set aside. Peel and slice peaches. Add remaining ingredients and toss lightly. Put into pie shell. Bake for 30 minutes. Make topping by mixing flour, sugar, and cinnamon. Cut butter into small cubes and cut into flour mixture. Remove pie from oven and spread topping on peaches. Return to oven and bake for an additional 15 minutes.

GOOD FRESH PEACHES COULD ALWAYS BE FOUND IN VIRGINIA IN LATE AUGUST. WE CANNED A LOT OF THEM, BUT WE TREATED OURSELVES TO FRESH PEACH PIE AS OFTEN AS WE COULD.

Edna Lewis

Madison's Temple

Looking at the Madison temple today, it is hard to imagine that it stands on the spot of the noisy, smelly blacksmith shop that served Montpelier. Upon his father's death, James Madison removed the shop and built the temple, which he intended to use for a study. William Thornton, architect of the Capitol, drew a sketch for Madison, and Thomas Jefferson suggested two carpenters—John Nelson and James Dinsmore—to build the structure. They dug a 24-foot hole and lined it with brick. The dirt removed from the hole covered the area where the blacksmith shop stood, and the hole became an ice house. Once the temple was built, James had blocks of ice cut from the several ponds located around the plantation. The ice was then hauled to the temple, lowered into the well, and covered with straw. James was sure that the ice would last to make mint juleps and ice cream all summer—certainly a luxury in 19th-century Virginia. His overseer thought this was folly. But James told him he'd serve him an iced mint julep on the Fourth of July and that the overseer would owe him a Christmas turkey if he did. James won his turkey.

Ice Cream

Ice cream graced the tables of the finest homes in England as early as the 15th century. And in the 18th century, while ice cream was not common, it was not unknown in America.

George Washington, who may have learned about ice cream from his good friend the Marquis de Lafayette, had an ice cream freezer as early as 1784. His guests enjoyed desserts made in this "cream machine for ice," and Mrs. Washington served ice cream and lemonade to the ladies who attended her parties. In Philadelphia, Mrs. John Adams ate ices to get cool, and Brannon's tea garden near Brooklyn sold ice cream.

It was Thomas Jefferson, however, who became enamored of ice cream and had the most influence on its popularity in America. While in France he discovered frozen cream recipes. He brought these recipes back to Virginia and is said to have served ice cream made from vanilla pods which he ordered from Paris in 1791. But ice cream was still a rare treat when Jefferson's friend, Dolley Madison, served it as the grand finale to a White House dinner.

Throughout the 18th and 19th centuries, ice cream was served in many forms. It was piled high in glasses or china cups, pressed into intricate pewter molds and turned out onto a plate, or spooned into a glacier that held crushed ice to keep the ice cream cold.

Ice cream molded in fruit shapes and decorated with the leaves of real greenery was very popular during the 18th century. Victorian times brought pillar molds that created concoctions suggesting mansard roofs and towers of Gothic revival architecture. Such fancy shapes remained in fashion until the turn of the 20th century when cozy domestic shapes became the rage once again.

Minted iced tea is certain to taste even better when served from a beloved cut crystal pitcher.

French Vanilla Ice Cream

This rich ice cream is delicious with the peach streusel pie.

4 egg yolks
1 cup sugar
1 teaspoon salt
2 cups milk

1 vanilla bean
1/4 cup vanilla extract
1 quart whipping cream

Beat egg yolks lightly. Add sugar and salt. Set aside. Split the vanilla bean, add to the milk, and pour into a saucepan. Heat until slightly scalded. Pour into a clean saucepan and add egg yolk mixture. Heat, stirring continuously, over medium heat for about 3-5 minutes, until the mixture coats a spoon. Remove from heat and strain into a bowl. Set bowl in larger bowl of ice water until mixture is cool. Add vanilla and whipping cream. Put in refrigerator and chill. When thoroughly chilled process in ice cream freezer according to the manufacturer's directions.

*M*AKING ICE CREAM WAS ALWAYS A FAMILY AFFAIR WHEN I WAS A CHILD. IT TOOK A LOT OF CHURNING, SO WE NEEDED A LOT OF HANDS. THINKING OF SUCH TIMES BRINGS BACK FOND MEMORIES. THREE CUPS OF ANY CRUSHED FRUIT CAN BE ADDED ONCE THE ICE CREAM BEGINS TO FREEZE.

Edna Lewis

Minted Iced Tea

You can have a bottomless pitcher of this tea all summer if you have a mint garden. Just be sure to grow it in containers or in a raised bed by itself. It is very invasive.

12 long pieces fresh mint
12 teaspoons loose tea
8 cups boiling water

2 cups sugar
6 lemons, juiced
2 quarts ice water

Strip leaves from mint and put in bowl with loose tea. Pour 4 cups boiling water over mint and tea. Let stand 15 minutes. Strain mixture. Mix together sugar and lemon juice with remaining 4 cups boiling water. Combine both mixtures and add ice water. To serve, fill glasses with ice and pour tea over ice. Do not put ice in the tea. Garnish with fresh mint.

Autumn

A faint chill in the air, a fiery-red evening sky, and smoke from wood-burning fires signal that autumn is arriving. The hills and mountains burst with color. Maple trees show off their russet and golden leaves. Wild grasses boast their

magnificent sand-colored plumes. Golden fields overflow with bales of hay. And blooming mums and asters keep color alive in the garden.

It is a time when everyone is busy. Grapes are ripe for picking. Crops must be harvested. Vines must be pruned. And foods are at their peak for curing, smoking, and preserving. These last weeks of summer, while the days are still warm and the evenings cool, are a wonderful time to invite a few guests to share the bounty of the harvest.

In the fall, corn cutting followed with a fervor, with everyone trying to catch the right weather so that the job could be completed. The corn was cut and stacked into shocks, each ear of corn was taken off the shock, and all the ears were piled up. Then men would come along with wagons and haul the ears into the corn house. Then my mother would serve them a meal of fried chicken, baked ham, roasted new potatoes, baked tomatoes, green beans, cake, and apple pie. They always promised to be back the next year. I'm sure the food had something to do with that.

Hog butchering, another big project, generally took place in early December. A good cold spell was essential because the hogs had to hang at least three days in the cold air before they could be cut up. We waited impatiently during those three days. The hogs had been fed the corn in the fall, as well as all the surplus milk and garden weeds and vegetables, which meant the dishes produced from them would be delicious. Once the hogs were butchered, their fat was cut off and rendered. Then began the making and curing of sausages, liver pudding, and souse, the salting and smoking of hams, bacon, and shoulders. It was a hectic time. Every family had more than a dozen hogs, so everyone joined in helping everyone else.

Edna Lewis

A Grape Harvest Festival

Early fall rings in the harvest on farms all around Piedmont Virginia. And the vineyards are no exception. Harvesting grapes requires a Herculean effort. So, once the harvest is over, everyone gathers for an informal celebration to enjoy the first wine of the season. The menu features subtly flavored Virginia wines and food featuring late harvest vegetables and herbs: chowder made from the last corn of the season, trout stuffed with wild mushrooms picked at their peak, the year's chestnut crop, and juicy ripe pears. Old wine barrels serve as side tables. Wine bottles filled with mums and grape leaves make enchanting centerpieces. Bales of hay provide seating. And the intricate purple and green fruit pattern of the Royal Ducal earthenware complements the theme.

At the end of the day, as the setting sun tints the sky, the sight of ducks on the pond with a backdrop of rolling hills evokes a sense of peace that is hard to describe.

A weathered antique table and grapevine chairs are set out in the vineyard after the grape harvest.

Barboursville

The spirit of Thomas Jefferson has lured vintners to Virginia. Gianni Zonin and his three brothers, who run Zonin family wineries in Italy, are among them. Fascinated by Jefferson and familiar with the early failure of winemaking in Virginia, the Zonins purchased this 850-acre estate and began planting varietal grapes.

Originally owned by James Madison's good friend, Virginia governor James Barbour, the property includes the ruins of a two-story brick mansion, built in 1814, that was destroyed by fire in 1884. The house, laid in Flemish bond, was designed by Thomas Jefferson in the Neoclassical style he so loved. Earthen ramps, rather than steps, led up to the columned portico. The center of the house features an octagonal two-story drawing room flanked on either side by a pair of square rooms separated by hallways. True to Jefferson's style, the stairways are tucked into these hallways.

Once the center of a large complex, the house was surrounded by dependencies, gardens, a mill, a racetrack, storehouses, shops, and a cemetery. A few of the dependencies still remain on the property. A pair of them, now joined into one building by a small brick section, was renovated and occupied by the Barbours after the mansion was destroyed. Just one room deep, the house sits in the slope to the west of the ruins. Columned porticos similar to those on the original mansion form the front of the house. Restored by Gianni Zonin and his wife, the house boasts many paintings, furnishings, and decorative objects from Europe, including 1800 English porcelain, 18th-century engravings, and an antique Venetian desk.

A Grape Harvest Festival

Menu

Smoked Trout and Corn Chowder

Field Greens with Red Grape Vinaigrette

Forest-Mushroom-Stuffed Trout

Black Walnut and Country Ham Brown Butter Sauce

Pork Loin Stuffed with Chestnuts

Savory Bread Pudding

Apple and Currant Chutney

Brussels Sprouts with Braised Chestnuts

Late Harvest Riesling Poached Pears

Chestnut Cake

Virginia Glogg

Local Virginia wines are a fine complement to any meal.

Virginia Glogg

As the sun sets on the horizon and brings a chill to the air, a cup of this old-fashioned wine drink will bring warmth to the soul.

2 quarts cabernet sauvignon
2 ounces dried orange peel
2 ounces cinnamon sticks
20 cardamom seeds
25 cloves
1 pound blanched almonds
1 pound seedless raisins
1 lump sugar
1 fifth brandy

Pour cabernet into a saucepan. Put orange peel, cinnamon sticks, cardamom seeds, and cloves in the center of a piece of cheesecloth and tie securely. Add to wine. Simmer for 15 minutes, stirring occasionally. Add almonds and raisins and boil an additional 15 minutes. Remove saucepan from stove and add sugar. Pour brandy over sugar. Stir and remove spice bag. Serve hot in mugs or punch cups.

OUR GARDEN PROMISES GRAPES AND FIGS IN ABUN-DANCE.

Dolley Madison

Smoked Trout and Corn Chowder

Smoked trout can be purchased from trout farms and specialty stores.

3 ears fresh corn
6 slices bacon
2 small onions
4 medium potatoes
2 cups chicken stock
1 cup half-and-half
8 ounces smoked trout
1/2 teaspoon fresh thyme
Salt and pepper

Cut corn off the cob. Cut bacon into 1-inch pieces. Peel and chop onions and potatoes. In heavy skillet, fry bacon over medium heat until crisp; remove and place bacon on paper towel. Sauté onion in bacon drippings until tender. Drain off excess drippings. In a heavy saucepan, cook potatoes in chicken stock until tender. Add onion, corn, half-and-half, smoked trout, and thyme. Season to taste with salt and pepper.

Winemaking in the Virginia Piedmont

Virginia planters were crushing native grapes for wine as early as 1609, but they found their results less than acceptable. Hoping to grow grapes that would produce European-style wines, they began importing grapevine roots from France. At the time, England was pressuring the colonies to produce a quality wine, and in 1619 the Virginia House of Burgesses passed Acte 12, which was the first of many legislative efforts to require planters to grow grapes for wine. While knowledgeable planters generally felt that native vines could be cultivated from European root stock, their attempts were generally unsuccessful. Unaware that their failure was due to delicate European vines that couldn't thrive in Virginia's cold winters and humid summers, most experienced planters stopped experimenting by the late 1700s.

Thomas Jefferson, however, was unwilling to give up. He offered Italian landowner and farmer Philip Mazzei 2,000 acres adjoining his Monticello on which to grow vines. But Mazzei had little success and returned to Italy. Undaunted, Jefferson continued to pursue his experiments, convinced that Virginia was indeed a good environment for growing grapes. It is doubtful, however, that he ever produced a drinkable wine.

By the 1800s, cross-pollination by bees of European and American grapes had resulted in hybrids that exhibited the finesse and complexity of the European grape along with the hardiness of the American variety. Wine production in Virginia began an upswing that peaked just before the Civil War. Unfortunately, few vineyards survived the war. Then in 1880, just as Southern counties were voting to prohibit alcohol, California wines began to flood the market and the demand for Virginia wine began to shrink. Production declined, and by 1914, when Virginia outlawed alcohol, very few vineyards remained. Attempts to plant grapes after Prohibition were unsuccessful, and expertise in grape growing and winemaking virtually disappeared.

It was not until 1970 that a few modern pioneers planted a small number of French hybrid vines that began a new era of wine production in Virginia.

Virginia produces world-class wine from both chardonnay and cabernet grapes.

Forest-Mushroom-Stuffed Trout with Black Walnut and Country Ham Brown Butter Sauce

There are few dishes that have more Virginia style than this lovely dish of local Virginia trout, forest mushrooms, country ham, and black walnuts.

2 cups cubed white bread	5 ribs celery, chopped
3 tablespoons olive oil	1/4 cup fresh thyme, chopped
2 pounds forest mushrooms	Salt and pepper
1/2 cup butter	1 cup chicken stock
2 onions, chopped	8 fresh trout fillets

Preheat oven to 450 degrees. Place bread cubes on a baking sheet and bake, stirring occasionally, until golden. Heat olive oil in a saucepan. Slice mushrooms and sear in hot olive oil until golden brown. Add butter, onion, and celery to the mushrooms. Cook until soft and tender. Add thyme and adjust seasoning with salt and pepper. Adjust the consistency with the chicken stock. Assemble stuffing and spread some on each fillet. Roll fillets into cylinders and secure with butcher's twine. Place fillets on a baking pan and bake for about 15 minutes. To serve, cut each filet into two pieces and put on serving plate. Surround with sauce.

For the sauce

4 tablespoons butter	1 tablespoon fresh lemon juice
1/4 cup julienned country ham	1 tablespoon parsley
	3 tablespoons chopped chives
1/4 cup black walnuts	1/4 teaspoon salt
1/4 cup heavy cream	1/8 teaspoon pepper

Melt butter in heavy skillet. Add ham and cook until butter turns a light brown. Add black walnuts and cream, and cook until slightly reduced and thickened. Add the lemon juice, parsley, and chives. Stir for a minute or two. Remove from heat and mix in the salt and black pepper.

*T*HE OUTER SHELL OF THE BLACK WALNUT IS SO HARD THAT IT IS ALMOST IMPOSSIBLE TO BREAK IT. WE HAD A BLACK WALNUT TREE, AND I REMEMBER MY AUNT PUTTING THE NUTS IN OUR DRIVEWAY AND BACKING THE CAR OVER THEM. THAT'S PROBABLY THE ONLY WAY TO BREAK THAT SHELL, SO I WOULD RECOMMEND BUYING BLACK WALNUTS THAT HAVE ALREADY BEEN SHELLED.

Edna Lewis

Field Greens with Red Grape Vinaigrette

The chestnuts provide an interesting texture to the field greens.

1 pound red grapes
1/2 cup red wine vinegar
2 tablespoons sugar
1/2 tablespoon salt
1/2 teaspoon pepper

2 cups olive oil
1 red onion, chopped
1/2 cup boiled chestnuts
4 cups mixed field greens

Wash grapes and purée in food processor. Strain. Combine purée, vinegar, sugar, salt, and pepper in food processor. Process, adding oil slowly in a steady stream. Add onion and correct seasoning. Set aside. Coarsely chop chestnuts and put on a baking sheet in one layer. Toast in 400-degree oven until golden. Place field greens in large bowl. Toss with vinaigrette. Add chestnuts and toss again.

Pork Loin Stuffed with Chestnuts

This flavorful dish is light on fat and bursting with taste. Chopped dried apricots make a nice addition to the stuffing.

5-pound boneless pork loin
1/2 cup celery, chopped
1 onion, chopped
1 tablespoon butter
1/2 pound ground pork
1 tablespoon chopped parsley
2 tablespoons brandy
1/2 teaspoon salt
1/2 teaspoon pepper

1/8 teaspoon allspice

For the sauce
2 tablespoons pork drippings
3 tablespoons flour
2 cups chicken stock
1 pound boiled chestnuts
1 teaspoon brandy
Salt and pepper

A chestnut-stuffed pork loin graces an heirloom Royal Ducal serving plate.

Have butcher butterfly pork loin. Pound lightly to even thickness. Cook celery and onion in butter until tender. Combine with ground pork, parsley, brandy, and seasonings. Spread over roast. Roll up roast and tie firmly. Roast in 350-degree oven until the meat thermometer reads 160 degrees. Remove from oven and let rest 10-15 minutes. Remove prok loin from the pan. Pour off extra fat from drippings, add flour, and cook for 1 minute. Add chicken stock and cook over medium heat, stirring until mixture thickens. Add chestnuts and brandy. Season to taste with salt and pepper. Serve with sauce on the side.

Preserving the Grape and Other Fruits of the Land

Southerners have been preserving food at home for centuries. Throughout the first half of the 19th century, preserved foods provided a major portion of their meals. And for decades after the Civil War, Southerners dried, salted, pickled, potted, canned, jellied, or otherwise preserved almost every kind of food.

Wild fruit was plentiful in the colonies. Long before the Europeans arrived, blackberries and muscadines—a variety of wild (or fox) grapes—were flourishing along the Eastern seaboard. Europeans who came to the South in the 17th century brought quince. And the sour little purple damson plums that ripen in Virginia in August and December are descendants of a fruit the British have enjoyed for centuries.

The colonists found that many of the wild fruits had to be very ripe to taste sweet, but when cooked with sugar, the tart muscadines, blackberries, quince, and damson plums tasted delicious. Thus, something very much like jam was probably cooking over colonial fires long before the American Revolution.

The earliest of cookbooks used in this country contained recipes for quince jelly. Jams and preserves from cherries, strawberries, and plums have been popular since antebellum days.

Clearly, making jams and jellies today holds a special attraction for cooks who enjoy exploring food in history and history in food. It takes some experience to master the art. Like any handmade product, it takes time, energy, and skill. So, while canning is not as commonplace today as it was in the early years of our country, it is popular among those who take pride in creating products that are superior in appearance and taste.

There is an abundance of vineyards in the foothills of the Blue Ridge Mountains in piedmont Virginia.

Apple and Currant Chutney

Refrigerated, this chutney will keep for several weeks.

1 pound Granny Smith apples
2 cups cider vinegar
2-1/2 cups sugar
1/2 cup fresh lemon juice
2 tablespoons ginger root
1 teaspoon salt
1 tablespoon mustard seeds
1 cup currants
8 cloves of garlic, peeled

Peel and quarter the apples. Combine vinegar and sugar
in a heavy saucepan. Bring to a boil. Add apples, lemon
juice, ginger root, salt, mustard seeds, and currants.
Bring to a boil and then simmer for about 45 minutes.
Put garlic cloves in food processor and pulse until
crushed. Stir into the chutney. Let cool and spoon into
sterilized jars.

*A jar of freshly canned chutney
sits amid fresh vegetables in a
grapevine basket.*

Savory Bread Pudding

*Try serving this bread pudding with some of the sauce made by the
pork loin.*

1 cup diced onions
1/2 cup chopped celery
2 tablespoons olive oil
1 loaf stale bread

2 tablespoons fresh sage,
  finely chopped
4 cups milk
1 egg, beaten
1 teaspoon salt

Preheat oven to 350 degrees. Cook onions and celery in olive
oil until soft. Cut crust off bread and tear into small pieces. Add
to onion and celery mixture. Add sage and toss gently until well
mixed. Heat milk to scalding point and add egg and salt. Pour
milk mixture over bread mixture and toss until well mixed. Pour
into buttered loaf pan and bake for about 20 minutes until a
knife blade inserted in the center of the pudding comes out
clean and the top is golden brown. Let cool slightly. Remove
from pan and slice.

APPLE AND CURRANT
CHUTNEY IS DELICIOUS
SERVED WITH PORK OR
GAME. IT CAN ALSO BE MADE
WITH PEARS OR PEACHES,
WHICH WILL BE EQUALLY
DELICIOUS.

Edna Lewis

Wine and Chestnuts

Nothing could be more fitting on a cold fall evening than roasting chestnuts and sharing a bottle of wine with good friends. The chestnuts, wine, and camaraderie blend well. Serendipitously, the chestnut season coincides with the release of the first fresh new red wines. And, as an example of nature's perfect timing, the two are wonderful complements to each other. The richness of the nut meat is a perfect baffle to the surprising undeveloped flavors of the fresh wine–the sum of the two being far greater and more rewarding than either alone.

There is no wine more fitting to enjoy with the roasted chestnuts than the first wine of the year. Known as the vino novello, Beaujolais nouveau, or Gamay nouveau, the wine is made in six weeks using an ultra-quick process that calls for placing whole grapes in carbon dioxide-filled tanks. This light, lively wine is fermented without the assistance of yeast, which is commonly used in making most other wines. The result is a wine that has the juicy fruitiness of just-picked grapes without the bitter tannic aftertaste. Its fruity bouquet has unmistakable overtones.

Bottled at the end of October and released around the first week of November, the vino novello does not last very well, but it does remain a decent drinking wine until Christmas. After that, although it is still palatable, it will have lost much of its youthful charm. So, New Year's Eve should see the end of the novello.

Most of the major French, Italian, and California wineries produce some type of novello. And, in recent years, a few Virginia wineries have followed suit. Among them, Villa Appalachia is producing a novello that combines their Sangiovese and Cabernet Franc.

Brussels Sprouts with Braised Chestnuts

This dish is greatly enhanced by the addition of a good veal glacé. You should be able to find it at any gourmet market.

2 pounds Brussels sprouts
1 tablespoon oil
2 tablespoons butter
2 pounds boiled chestnuts
1/2 cup chopped onions

1 cup port wine
2 teaspoons chopped thyme
5 cups chicken stock
1/2 cup veal glacé
Salt and pepper

Trim Brussels sprouts and score at the stem. Place oil, butter, chestnuts, and onions in a hot saucepan. When onions are slightly brown and translucent, deglaze the pan with the port wine. Add thyme, Brussels sprouts, chicken stock, veal glacé, and salt and pepper. Cover and cook until most of the liquid is absorbed and the chestnuts and Brussels sprouts are tender.

The grape pattern on the vintage Royal Ducal plate complements the champagne grapes served with the poached pear.

Late Harvest Riesling Poached Pears

The best time for this dish is fall, when the fall Bartlett pears are sweet and full of flavor.

6 firm Bartlett pears
1-1/2 cups late harvest Riesling
1 cup water
1 cup lemon juice
1/2 cup sugar

1 teaspoon orange zest
1 teaspoon lemon zest
1 cinnamon stick
1 piece star anise

Combine Riesling, water, sugar, orange and lemon zest, lemon juice, and spices in a medium pan. Bring to a boil. Reduce heat to low. Add pears to liquid. Cover pears with a plate to keep them submerged. Simmer for 20 minutes or until pears can be pierced with a fork.

*A*T THIS MOMENT WE HAVE ONLY THREE AND TWENTY GUESTS.

Dolley Madison

Chestnut Cake

This elegant, rich cake is good any time.

2 pounds fresh or flash-frozen chestnuts
1-1/2 sticks butter
1 cup sugar
4 eggs, separated
2 tablespoons rum
2/3 cup heavy cream
1 teaspoon vanilla
2 tablespoons sugar
1/4 cup apricot jam

WE HAD GREAT FUN COOKING CHESTNUTS IN THE FIREPLACE WHEN WE WERE CHILDREN. NOW WHEN I SEE CHESTNUTS COMING INTO THE MARKET IN THE FALL, I THINK FONDLY ABOUT HOME AND OUR FIREPLACE.

Edna Lewis

Score flat side of chestnuts with point of knife. Place nuts in saucepan, cover with boiling water, and simmer for about 1/2 hour until soft. Test by cutting one in half. Cool and peel while hot. They become difficult to peel when cold. Put chestnuts through a food mill. Measure 2 cups, using a light touch. Cream butter, adding sugar gradually until mixture is light and fluffy. Add beaten egg yolks to butter mixture and mix well. Add rum and grated chestnuts. Mix well. Beat egg whites stiff but not dry. Gently fold them into cake batter. Spoon into two 8-inch layer cake pans with removable bottoms and bake at 350 degrees for 25 minutes. Remove from oven and slip off rims. Set on rack to cool. When cakes are cold, remove bottoms. Whip heavy cream with the vanilla and 2 tablespoons sugar. Spread on first layer. Cover with second layer and spread top with apricot jam.

For the chocolate glaze
1 square baker's chocolate
1 tablespoon butter
1 tablespoon sugar

Combine the chocolate and butter in a saucepan. Place over hot water and stir until chocolate has melted and the mixture is smooth. Add sugar and stir well. Dribble over top and sides of cake.

A Breakfast After the Hunt

With the holidays not far ahead, Virginians turn their thoughts to the hunt. The dogwood sports a crimson red, and the countryside is scarlet with the hunters. After the hunt, there is no better way to fortify the saddle-weary hunter than to offer a hearty repast.

The term breakfast to the hunter actually means something different from what we would normally imagine. It could be a lunch or a brunch, an elaborate affair, or an alfresco picnic. Two prerequisites, however, are heartiness and camaraderie. Its purpose is to restore the weary chasers after the hunt. And it is as much an event as it is a meal.

The hunt breakfast is old-fashioned Southern. It is also country, not just because of the menu but because of its presentation, which calls for copper, earthenware crocks, and old baskets.

A huge bouquet of wildflowers takes center stage on an 18th-century serving table. Surrounding a steaming pot of Brunswick stew are striking handmade baskets chock full of fragrant warm biscuits, crusty breads, and the last harvest of fruit.

The rest of the menu reflects the Old Dominion: green tomato and sausage tart, smoked Virginia trout cakes, country ham, spoon bread, and biscuits. It is a menu that can be prepared ahead. One that will satisfy the heartiest of appetites. And one that perpetuates a sporting tradition.

An 18th-century dining table is set with imported Chinese porcelain and ivory-handled flatware that belonged to President Zachary Taylor.

Berry Hill

As its name implies, Berry Hill sits high on a hill in Orange County, overlooking pastures, vineyards, and meadows. The driveway leading to the rear of this stately house winds through lush vineyards, undulating fields of wheat and corn, and vast meadows of grazing cattle.

Deeded by Colonel James Taylor II to his son Zachary, grandfather of the President, Berry Hill was conveyed to his daughter, Elizabeth, and her husband, Thomas Bell, in 1762. The Bells subsequently sold the property to Reynolds Chapman and his wife Rebecca Conway Madison, the daughter of James Madison's brother William.

At that time, the plantation house was a story-and-a-half frame dwelling. By the mid-1820s, the Chapmans increased their land holdings and commissioned a home in a grander style. Built by craftsmen who had worked on the University of Virginia, Berry Hill, with its pedimented Tuscan portico on top of an arcade, strongly resembled one of the pavilions at the University. The woodworking throughout Berry Hill and its triple-hung windows show strong Jeffersonian influence as well.

Designed in a side-hall plan, the house is constructed of brick in Flemish bond on the front and American bond on the back and sides. The second-story portico was enclosed a few years after the house was built and windows on the east side were closed up. Somewhat later, a two-story west wing and a rear kitchen wing were added.

A Breakfast After the Hunt

Menu

Spicy Bloody Marys

Hot Curried Fruit

Country Style Venison Paté with Bourbon-Grained Mustard

Smoked Trout Cakes with Horseradish Cream

Green Tomato and Sausage Tart

Brunswick Stew

Virginia Country Ham

Sweet Potato Biscuits

Southern Greens

Virginia Spoon Bread

Old-Fashioned Bourbon Cake

Fox Hunting

The history of fox hunting in Virginia dates back to colonial days. The fox, always the farmer's enemy, was overrunning the countryside in those early days of our country. Despised as vermins and thieves, foxes were impossible to keep out of chicken coops. So began hunting the fox.

George Washington, probably the best-known hunter of all time, was introduced to fox hunting by Lord Thomas Fairfax, who settled in Virginia in 1746. Fairfax was a devoted fox hunter who brought his horses and hounds with him from England. Washington spent a great deal of time and effort breeding his own hounds and riding with guests who visited Mount Vernon. Jefferson was also an enthusiastic and capable hunter.

Today, although fox hunting is treated as more of a sport of tradition than in colonial days (the fox himself is not captured), it still adheres to the strict protocol established more than 200 years ago. And it remains an exciting sport for which it is easy to become an avid, lifelong enthusiast.

Spicy Bloody Marys

This mix also makes a delicious nonalcoholic drink. Just replace the beer with a nonalcoholic brand and replace the vodka with tonic.

1 quart spicy tomato juice	10-20 drops Tabasco sauce
8 ounces beef bouillon	1 tablespoon horseradish
4 ounces beer	1/2 teaspoon coarse pepper
	12 ounces vodka

Pour juice and bouillon into large pitcher. Add beer, hot sauce, and horseradish. Mix well and stir in vodka. Serve in tall glasses filled with ice. Garnish with stalk of celery or freshly picked lovage.

Hot Curried Fruit

You can give this dish more of a Virginia flavor by using Damson plums.

4 apples, peeled	8 dark purple plums
4 oranges, peeled	1 lemon, juiced
4 pears, peeled	2 tablespoons curry powder
1 cup red seedless grapes	1/3 cup unsalted butter
1 cup white seedless grapes	1/2 cup light brown sugar

Preheat oven to 325 degrees. Core apples. Slice fruit and put in large bowl. Toss with lemon juice. Mix curry powder and brown sugar together and mix with fruit. Put in greased baking dish and dot with butter. Cover and bake for about 45 minutes. Uncover and cook for another 15 minutes until fruit is soft. Serve warm.

Smoked Trout Cakes

*You can smoke your own trout according to directions for smoking
game hens in the preceding chapter.*

12 ounces smoked trout
2 teaspoons capers
1/2 teaspoon grated lemon peel
2 tablespoons scallions, chopped

1/8 teaspoon black pepper
1 egg, beaten
1/4 cup heavy cream
1/2 cup bread crumbs

Remove skin from trout and break fish into small pieces. Combine with capers, grated lemon peel, scallions, and pepper. Toss well. Add egg, cream, and bread crumbs. Form mixture into cakes and roll cakes in remaining bread crumbs. Coat a large sauté pan with oil. Heat over medium heat until hot. Add cakes and sauté until nicely browned on each side, about 2-3 minutes per side.

THE PROFUSION OF MY TABLE SO REPUGNANT TO FOREIGN CUSTOMS ARISES FROM THE HAPPY CIRCUMSTANCES OF ABUNDANCE AND PROSPERITY IN OUR COUNTRY.

Dolley Madison

Horseradish Cream

8 ounces sour cream
1/4 cup fresh horseradish, grated
1/8 teaspoon white pepper
1/8 teaspoon black pepper
1/2 teaspoon salt
1/4 teaspoon paprika
1/2 teaspoon garlic, minced

Combine above ingredients and
mix well.

*An 18th-century birdcage Windsor
chair invites a weary hunter to rest
by a blazing fire.*

Breakfast

The hearty breakfast harks back to the Southern plantation when heartiness was considered the proper way to be hospitable to guests who stayed the night. Often the most important meal of the day, plantation breakfasts were generally so luxurious that guest after guest described them in detail to others.

The tradition of a substantial breakfast carried over to the late 18th and 19th centuries. For the leisure and laboring classes alike, the first meal of the day in those times was often extensive and substantial, if not elaborate. There are stories in every Southern state of breakfast feasts for social occasions such as fox hunts and horse races, for house guests who happened through, and for families preparing for a long day in the fields. And while the food grew lighter through the years, the meal remained plentiful. Today, because of stricter schedules and a trend toward eating lighter, breakfast has become a trimmed-down version of its former self. For many Americans, a stop at a fast-food outlet for a pastry and coffee has become standard. And a first-rate breakfast is hard to find.

But country inns and bed-and-breakfast inns have reintroduced the tradition of the substantial early morning meal. A delicious morning repast shared with good company or lingered over alone with the morning paper is a pleasure that should be experienced rather than merely remembered.

A Queen Anne corner chair sits by an antique pine hutch.

Country Style Venison Paté

Although a bit time consuming, this paté is well worth the effort. It is an elegant appetizer and makes a satisfying accompaniment when served with French bread.

1 pound cubed pork butt	1/8 teaspoon allspice
1 pound cubed venison	1/2 teaspoon thyme
4 ounces pork fat	1/2 teaspoon basil
4 garlic cloves	1/8 cup bourbon
2 eggs	1 small green apple, diced
1/8 teaspoon ginger	16 slices thick bacon

Preheat oven to 350 degrees. Line a loaf pan with bacon. Grind pork, pork fat, and venison with garlic. Combine meat mixture with remaining ingredients. Pack mixture in bacon-lined loaf pan. Cover loosely with foil. Bake for 1 hour. Remove foil and cook another 30 minutes until the paté turns a golden brown. Weight down with a foil-covered brick and let cool. Cover tightly with plastic wrap and refrigerate at least 8 hours. To serve, slice and grill. Garnish with assorted greens, melba toast, and grain mustard.

Brunswick Stew

Traditional Brunswick stew was made with squirrel or rabbit, but many modern recipes have substituted chicken.

1 chicken, 3 to 3-1/2 pounds	2 cups lima beans
5 quarts water	2 cups corn
1/2 pound smoked bacon	1 teaspoon fresh thyme
4 cups tomatoes	2 teaspoons salt
6 potatoes	1 teaspoon black pepper
1 large onion	

Cut chicken into serving pieces. Cut bacon into thin strips. Peel, seed, and chop tomatoes. Cube potatoes and dice onion. Place bacon strips in large stock pot. Add onion and sauté until translucent. Add water and chicken and simmer for 2 hours. Add tomato, lima beans, corn, potatoes, thyme, salt, and pepper. Cook for about 30 minutes longer, stirring frequently to avoid sticking. Adjust seasoning if necessary.

Brunswick stew is served in a whimsical tureen.

Bourbon-Grained Mustard

This mustard is far superior to any commercial brand. It is a nice compliment to the paté.

1/3 cup yellow mustard seed	1/2 teaspoon coriander seed
1/3 cup black mustard seed	1-1/2 teaspoons salt
4 whole cloves	5/8 cup bourbon
1/2 teaspoon anise seed	5/8 cup cider vinegar
1/2 teaspoon peppercorns	

Grind dry ingredients using coffee mill or other type mill. Add liquid ingredients. Allow at least 8 hours before serving.

THERE WERE A LOT OF SMALL CORNFIELDS NEAR OUR HOME. MOST OF THEM WERE SURROUNDED BY WOODS WHICH MEANT THAT THERE WERE ALWAYS SQUIRRELS THERE. MY BROTHER WOULD BRING HIS RIFLE ALONG WHEN WE WENT TO PICK CORN. WE WOULD THEN USE THEM IN BRUNSWICK STEW, BUT WE ALSO LIKE THEM STEWED BY THEMSELVES. THEY WERE MUCH SWEETER THAN RABBIT.

Edna Lewis

Green Tomato and Sausage Tart

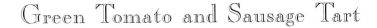

At the end of the season, we always had more tomatoes on the vines than could possibly ripen before the frost. So we gathered them to make chow-chow pickles and green tomato preserves. Sometimes mother would wrap them in tissue paper and store them in the dark cellar to proudly surprise us with them during hog-killing season.

Edna Lewis

This tart travels well and can be served at room temperature without losing any of its flavor.

For the cornmeal crust
2/3 cup white cornmeal
1-1/3 cups all-purpose flour
1 teaspoon salt
3/4 cup butter
3 tablespoons ice water

For the tart
1 pound country sausage
3 teaspoons sage, chopped

1 teaspoon cayenne pepper
1/4 teaspoon black pepper
2 cups chopped scallions
2 cups heavy whipping cream
2 green tomatoes, sliced
1/8 cup honey
1 teaspoon cider vinegar

Place cornmeal in heavy skillet. Toast over medium heat, stirring constantly. When cornmeal is a nice butternut brown, take off heat. Let cool. Combine cooled cornmeal with flour and salt. Cut butter into mixture with fingers or pastry cutter until mixture resembles coarse meal. Add enough ice water to form a soft dough. Mix with fork until mixture leaves sides of the bowl. Shape into a ball and flatten. Wrap in plastic and refrigerate for 30 minutes. Roll out on floured board and lay in a 10-inch tart shell. Trim excess and pierce bottom with a fork. Bake at 350 degrees for 8 minutes. Let cool. Crumble sausage into a bowl. Add sage, cayenne, and black pepper. Mix well and let sit for 15 minutes. Sauté sausage in a heavy skillet over medium heat. Drain off any liquid. Add 1 cup chopped scallions and cook for 5 minutes. Add heavy cream. Add sausage mixture. Bring mixture to a boil and reduce until thick. Remove from heat and cool. Add remaining scallions to sausage mixture. Spoon into cooled tart crust. Arrange tomato slices over top in single layer. Mix honey and cider vinegar together and brush over tomatoes. Bake at 450 degrees for 10 minutes. Reduce oven to 350 degrees and bake for 30 minutes or until tomatoes are glazed.

A hearty green tomato and sausage tart is served on a rustic pewter plate.

Virginia Spoon Bread

Spoon bread is an old Virginia favorite that is meant to be spooned out of the casserole and eaten with a fork.

2-1/2 cups milk
1 cup cornmeal
4 eggs, separated
2 tablespoons butter

1/2 teaspoon baking powder
1 teaspoon sugar
1 teaspoon salt

Preheat oven to 375 degrees. Grease a 2-quart round baking dish. Scald milk and slowly stir cornmeal into scalded milk. Cook over low heat, stirring constantly, until mixture is the consistency of soft oatmeal. Remove from heat and stir in butter. Beat egg yolks. Add baking powder, sugar, salt, and egg yolks. Whip egg whites and gently fold into batter. Bake in a well-greased dish for about 25 minutes until puffed and brown. Serve immediately.

*T*HE SPOON BREAD THAT I REMEMBER FROM ORANGE COUNTY HAS A LIGHTER TEXTURE BECAUSE IT IS MADE WITH GRATED FRESH CORN THAT IS BLENDED TO A LIQUID STATE.

Edna Lewis

Dolley and Mr. Jefferson

James and Dolley's long, close friendship with Thomas Jefferson lasted more than 50 years. It began in the late 1700s and continued when, as Governor of Virginia, Jefferson asked Madison to serve as one of his official advisors and when, as President, he appointed Madison his Secretary of State. James and Dolley lived with Jefferson in the President's Mansion for a short time after they arrived at the Capital City. And they had their own bedroom at Monticello, Jefferson's Virginia home just 25 miles from Montpelier.

At the time of Jefferson's presidency, it was customary for female guests to be received by a hostess. Since both Jefferson and his Vice President were widowers, he asked Dolley to serve as hostess at various presidential functions. Her charming manner proved to be an asset at presidential events.

Thomas Jefferson, a bit less formal than his predecessors, shunned the ceremonial requirements expected of dignitaries of the time. He discontinued formal receptions and made himself available to anyone who wanted to see him. He chose to walk or ride

horseback rather than take a carriage. He met senators and congressmen dressed informally, often looking a bit disheveled.

Foreign dignitaries were stunned by Jefferson's informal manner, and it didn't take long for his informality to raise eyebrows. At state dinners, Jefferson paid little attention to formal procedures for entering a dining room, ranks of guests, and seating arrangements, often commenting that he followed a "pell mell" etiquette. Dolley, however, was constantly at his side to soothe any ruffled feathers.

COOKED WILD OR GARDEN GREENS WERE PART OF EVERY MEAL WHILE I WAS GROWING UP. THEY WERE THOUGHT TO BE VERY GOOD FOR YOU AND WERE OFTEN GIVEN FOR NOURISHMENT WHEN WE WERE SICK.

Edna Lewis

Southern Greens

If you boil your country ham, you can cook these greens in its liquor. Just be sure to cook in an uncovered pan or the greens will turn dark.

2 pounds smoked pork
6 quarts water
6 pounds mixed greens
Salt and freshly ground pepper

Cook the pork in water until very tender, about 2 hours. Remove meat. Clean collards, mustard greens, turnip greens. Dry thoroughly on towel. Add greens and cook uncovered over medium heat for about 20 minutes. Season to taste with salt and pepper.

Country Ham

Given that pigs were raised for food more than 2,000 years ago, it is not surprising to find that many countries have long and proud ham traditions. So, of course, does the United States, especially the Southeastern region.

Around Smithfield, Virginia, it is claimed that English hogs fattened on African peanuts and cured by Native American methods of salting and smoking were the source of the first Smithfield hams. As early as 1650, hams were being exported to Europe, and by the end of the 18th century the cured ham was widely praised as a coveted Southern delicacy. The earliest collections of recipes contained instructions (from Southern colonists) for salting, smoking, and aging hams, as well as for cooking them. Practically every farm and plantation included the tribal ritual of hog killing in its winter activities, and most of the meat they ate consisted of ham, bacon, and sausage from their smokehouses.

There are two kinds of Virginia hams: Williamsburg hams that are aged for seven to eight months, and Smithfield hams that are aged more than a year. Both are salted after slaughtering, coated with black pepper, smoked with hardwood, and hung up to age. However, hams from the peanut-fed Smithfield hogs absorb more salt and smoke, which gives them a distinct texture and flavor. The Smithfield ham thus became the standard by which all hams are measured, and the use of the name Smithfield on any ham raised outside the territorial boundaries is prohibited by Virginia law.

Customarily, hams were aged a year or more, and any ham taken from the smokehouse before eight or nine months was considered deficient. But modern times brought new methods, and the real country ham became a lost art. Today, however, interest in old country hams is returning and there can be found Smithfield hams that are peanut-fed, dry-salted, hickory-smoked, and aged for at least eight months.

Virginia Ham

Virginia hams get their unique flavor from being cured in dry salt as opposed to salt brine.

Scrub ham well, cover with cold water and soak for at least 72 hours. Change water every 8 hours. Remove from water and scrape off any mold. Bake or boil ham according to instructions below. When cooked, remove skin and save liquid. Trim fat, but leave a thin coat so there will be a white line on each slice. Slice in very thin slices always.

For baked ham
Place ham in roaster with 10 cups of water. Cover roaster and place in oven set at 500 degrees. Bake for 30 minutes. Turn oven off. Wait three hours. Turn oven back on at 500 degrees for another 20 minutes. Turn oven off again and leave about 8 hours. Do not open oven door once the roaster has been put in the oven until after this 8-hour period. Then remove ham from oven and uncover. When cool, drain liquid and let cool.

For boiled ham
Set in large pot and cover with water. Bring to a boil and let simmer slowly for at least 5 hours. The ham is cooked when bubbles filled with fat cover the skin. Remove from water and set on a rack over a large tray to cool.

I AM PARTIAL TO SMITHFIELD HAMS. THEY ARE CURED FOR A YEAR OR LONGER AND HAVE A MORE SMOKEY FLAVOR THAN THOSE AGED FOR LESS TIME.

Edna Lewis

Kite's hams hang ready for market in their curing house in Wolftown, Virginia.

A bourbon cake is topped with toasted walnuts and caramel.

Sweet Potato Biscuits

Biscuits made with sweet potatoes are amazingly moist and tender.

3 cups all-purpose flour
1/2 teaspoon baking soda
2 tablespoons baking powder
1/2 teaspoon cinnamon
1/2 teaspoon nutmeg
2 tablespoons butter

3 cups cooked mashed sweet
  potatoes
1 cup buttermilk
Pinch of brown sugar
Pinch of salt

Preheat oven to 400 degrees. Sift together flour, baking soda, baking powder, cinnamon, and nutmeg. Cut in butter with pastry blender or fingers until mixture resembles coarse meal. In separate bowl, combine sweet potatoes, buttermilk, brown sugar, and salt. Add to dry ingredients. Mix until well combined. Knead about 10 times and roll out to about an inch thickness. Cut out with biscuit cutter. Place on a ungreased baking sheet and bake for about 15 minutes.

Old-Fashioned Bourbon Cake

A RICH, HEAVY CAKE SO POPULAR IN THE SOUTH, THIS CAKE WILL STAY FRESH FOR SEVERAL DAYS IF KEPT UNDER A GLASS COVER. WHEN IT HAS PASSED ITS PRIME, SLICE AND TOAST IT AND SERVE IT WITH ICE CREAM OR ANY BRANDIED OR CURRIED FRUIT.

Edna Lewis

Substituting English walnuts for the Brazil nuts will give an interesting flavor to this cake.

1 cup butter
2 cups sugar
4 eggs
1 egg yolk
3 cups all-purpose flour

1/2 teaspoon salt
1/2 teaspoon ground mace
1 teaspoon baking powder
1 cup bourbon
8 ounces ground Brazil nuts

Put butter into a bowl and beat until creamy. Add sugar and beat until light and fluffy. Add eggs and extra yolk, one at a time, beating after each addition. Mix 1 cup of flour with salt, mace, and baking powder. Add to mixture, and beat well. Alternately add bourbon and remaining flour, beginning and ending with the flour. Mix in ground nuts. Pour into tube pan whose bottom has been greased and floured. Set in a cold oven. Bake at 275 degrees for 30 minutes, 300 degrees for another 30 minutes, and 325 degrees for 15 minutes. Remove from oven and turn onto wire rack to cool.

A Family Gathering at Thanksgiving

Along with fallen leaves crunching underfoot and soft, snugly sweaters, a crackling fire is one of autumn's most sensuous pleasures. And by the time Thanksgiving arrived on the plantation, fires were blazing in every room and the entire household was busy preparing for the beginning of the holiday season. As it is today, Thanksgiving on a Virginia plantation was a time for drawing family and friends together, a time for spirited toasting and feasting.

Families from far and near gathered together. And on a brisk November day, nothing could be more fitting than a splendid meal. Reminiscent of an earlier time, Thanksgiving dinner features a resplendent spread of traditional Virginia cuisine based on old family recipes—roasted turkey, mashed potatoes, giblet gravy, cranberries, cornbread, mincemeat, pumpkin, and, of course, chestnuts. The atmosphere is friendly and warm. And everyone is encouraged to linger.

Created here is a typical Thanksgiving Day dinner with updated versions of foods served in antebellum days. The table is set with antique Staffordshire and centered with an autumnal still life of fall fruits, vegetables, and nuts that bring seasonal color inside.

A handpainted mural on the dining room walls depicts the Virginia plantation.

Woodley

Driving up the long tree-lined allee, the perfectly proportioned Woodley, with its two identical wings, comes into view. Woodley was deeded by James Madison, Sr. to his son Ambrose, brother of the President. Ambrose, who was very close to his brother, built Woodley on land adjacent to Montpelier. His daughter, Nelly Conway, was Madison's favorite niece. She lived at Woodley all her life and was known to be a sensible outgoing woman who made a point of being at Montpelier for every family occasion. She was so close to her uncle that the large tree in her front yard was called "the President's oak" because his horse, Liberty, was often tied there while he visited.

The oldest portion of the house is a story-and-a-half central section, which was probably a hall and parlor dwelling with a chimney at either end. The 19th-century doorway has elaborate side-lights and a 13-pane transom, which are said to represent the original 13 colonies. The wainscoting and mantels in this section appear to be Federal, suggesting the house was remodeled in the early 19th century. Nelly Madison Willis, Ambrose's daughter, added the two flanking two-story wings in 1840. These wings extend slightly beyond the 18th-century house, and a gallery porch across the older structure provides access to all three sections. A late 18th-century kitchen and smokehouse still stand behind the house. The house is a showpiece of antiques, artwork, and objects.

A Family Gathering at Thanksgiving

Menu

Butternut and Acorn Squash Bisque with Chestnut Cream

Roasted Turkey with Oyster and Chestnut Stuffing

Toasted Pecan Wild Rice Stuffing

Cornbread and Country Sausage Dressing

Baked Yams and Granny Smith Apples

Garlic Mashed Potatoes

Giblet Gravy

Long-Cooked Green Beans

Orange-Cranberry Chutney

Mincemeat Pie

Caramel-Pumpkin Custard

Hot Toddies

Butternut and Acorn Squash Bisque with Chestnut Cream

This is an absolutely delicious fall soup. The flavor of the squash is enhanced by a touch of nutmeg. Be sure to use only freshly ground nutmeg as there is an enormous difference in flavor between it and the store-bought ground version.

Fresh thyme garnishes a bowl of butternut and acorn squash bisque.

2 butternut squash
1 acorn squash
1/4 cup water
1 medium onion
1/4 cup olive oil
2 quarts chicken stock
2 cups fresh orange juice
2 teaspoons dry sherry
1/4 teaspoon salt
1/8 teaspoon pepper
2 teaspoons ground
   nutmeg

Preheat oven to 350 degrees. Peel and dice squash. Put in baking dish. Pour 1/4 cup water around squash. Bake until soft. Dice onion and sauté in olive oil until soft. Add sherry, orange juice, and stock. Bring to boil for 2 minutes. Add squash, salt, pepper, and nutmeg. Simmer for 5 minutes. Turn off heat and purée with hand blender. Return to saucepan and reheat. Pour into bowls. Top with dollop of chestnut cream.

Chestnut Cream

1/4 cup roasted chestnuts
1/2 cup sour cream
1/2 cup heavy cream

Peel chestnuts and pulse in food processor until fine. Combine sour cream and heavy cream. Fold in chestnuts.

THE FAMILY HERE ARE AS THEY ALWAYS ARE, MOST AFFECTIONATE AND KIND . . .
Dolley Madison

Oyster-Chestnut Stuffing

For a nice light stuffing, select day-old bread and cornbread and toss lightly once the ingredients are together.

2 sticks butter
1 cup onion, diced
1 cup celery, diced
1 pint fresh oysters, chopped
1 tablespoon sage, chopped
1 tablespoon parsley, chopped

1 teaspoon ginger
4 cups day-old white bread
4 cups cornbread
1/4 cup chicken stock
1 cup roasted chestnuts
Salt and pepper

Crumble white bread and cornbread. Melt butter in a saucepan and sauté onions and celery until tender. Add oysters and cook lightly just until they begin to curl. Add herbs and cornbread and cook until flavors are well melded. Add chicken stock and bread. Heat well. Peel and chop chestnuts and add to mixture. Correct seasoning if necessary. Mix lightly but thoroughly. Put in turkey and bake.

OYSTERS WERE A MAINSTAY OF OUR HOLIDAY DINNERS. THEY ALWAYS SEEMED TO APPEAR, ALREADY SHUCKED AND IN BARRELS, IN OUR COUNTRY STORE AT CHRISTMASTIME. WE LOVED THEM ANY WAY MOTHER WOULD FIX THEM.

Edna Lewis

Large candles and scattered nuts make an eye-catching centerpiece for a Thanksgiving table.

Antebellum Thanksgivings

The very first Thanksgiving was actually celebrated in Jamestown, Virginia, as early as 1619, two years earlier than the more well-known celebration that took place in Massachusetts. However, it wasn't until 1777 that a national day of Thanksgiving was proclaimed. Spurred by the defeat of British General John Burgoyne, which marked a turning point in the Revolutionary War, a day of "solemn Thanksgiving and praise" for the success was declared by the Continental Congress in 1777. Then, in 1789, George Washington officially proclaimed a national day of Thanksgiving and Thomas Jefferson proclaimed a day of Thanksgiving in Virginia.

By 1860, Thanksgiving was being celebrated in most of the Southeastern states, and in 1863, Abraham Lincoln proclaimed a nationwide Thanksgiving Day be celebrated annually. Thanksgiving had at last become an institution, and although each state had its own special customs, huge feasts were the earmark of every one.

It is hard to imagine the opulence of Thanksgiving in the 19th century. More than 30 people often arrived for a dinner that typically consisted of as many as 10 meats. Pyramids of fresh fruit centered a table filled with the season's bounty. The place of honor was always held by a golden roasted wild turkey stuffed with a concoction of bread coarsely crumbled and seasoned with celery, pepper, and onion. Next to it sat great bowls of gravy heavy with giblets, covered dishes of snowy whipped potatoes, celery hearts, hot slaw, and huge bowls of custard, rich with cream and eggs, and seasoned with nutmeg.

As gracious gentlemen joined their charming ladies bedecked in silks and jewels, they raised their cups to toast a way of life they never dreamed

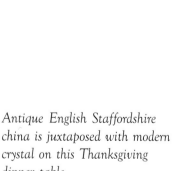

Antique English Staffordshire china is juxtaposed with modern crystal on this Thanksgiving dinner table.

Cornbread and Country Sausage Dressing

Bake this dressing in a separate pan and serve alongside the turkey with its stuffing.

1 pound country sausage	3 teaspoons sage, chopped
2 tablespoons butter	1 egg, beaten
3/4 cup onion, chopped	4 cups day-old cornbread,
3/4 cup celery, diced	crumbled
1 garlic clove, minced	Salt
1 teaspoon thyme, chopped	Cracked black pepper

Preheat oven to 350 degrees. Crumble sausage in a skillet. Cook until browned, about 5 minutes. Drain and set aside. Melt butter in same skillet. Add onion, celery, and garlic. Sauté over medium heat for 2-3 minutes. Transfer to large bowl. Add sausage, thyme, sage, and egg. Stir well. Add cornbread. Stir well and season to taste. Put in ovenproof dish and bake for 30 minutes.

A collection of birdhouses is displayed on a stone fireplace.

Orange~Cranberry Chutney

This is a pleasant change from the ubiquitous cranberry sauce.

3 cups fresh cranberries
3 oranges, peeled and chopped
1 cup sugar
1/2 cup water
1/2 cup orange juice
1 cup walnuts, chopped

Combine cranberries, oranges, sugar, water, and orange juice. Bring to a boil over high heat. Reduce heat to medium and cook for 10 minutes. Let cool to room temperature. Add walnuts to mixture and stir.

WE ALWAYS SEEMED TO HAVE A LARGE VARIETY OF CHUTNEYS, PRESERVES, AND PICKLES ON THE TABLE, ESPECIALLY IN WINTER WHEN FRESH VEGETABLES WERE SCARCE. THIS HAS STAYED WITH ME AND I STILL TRY TO PUT UP BERRIES AND FRUITS EACH YEAR WHEN I GET HOME TO ORANGE.

Edna Lewis

Family Ties

Family was the backbone of the Madisons throughout their lives. Both James and Dolley were very fond of their relatives and welcomed them into their home at all times. This devotion to family assured that the Madisons rarely had Montpelier to themselves. Dolley even shared the management of Montpelier's household with her mother-in-law, Nelly Madison.

A trusted confidante and dear friend to everyone in both families, Dolley and James were especially close to her sisters, Anna and Lucy, and her brother John. From age 14, Anna lived with Dolley and became her ward and closest companion. The two sisters were so close that when Anna married Richard Cutts and moved to Maine, Dolley was visibly distraught. Throughout her married years, Anna and her family spent months at a time with Dolley and James, actually living in the President's Mansion the year James was elected President.

Dolley's sister Lucy also spent several years living in the President's Mansion after the death of her husband. Her wedding to Justice Thomas Todd was the first to take place there. Brother John moved his family to a small farm near Montpelier and even lived a year at the President's Mansion during the winter of 1812. For years, he acted as Madison's secretary, taking dictation at Madison's request. His handwriting can be found throughout Madison's papers.

James was also extremely close to his older brother Ambrose, a trusted colleague, and his two eldest sisters, Nelly and Sarah. Madison's relationships with Ambrose and his sisters were warm, but that was not the case with brother William. Much younger than James, William did share his brother's political interests, but a definite uneasiness existed between them.

Upon his marriage to Dolley, James inherited guardianship of her son, John Payne Todd. Both a gambler and drinker, Payne ran up enormous debts. But Dolley still loved and doted on him. Her initial acceptance to Madison's marriage proposal was that James would be a protector of her beloved son. And that he was. James took him under his tutelage, even creating several diplomatic positions for him in an effort to help further Payne's career. And often, without Dolley's knowledge, he paid the enormous debts Payne ran up as a result of his heavy drinking and gambling.

Table and chairs that belonged to James and Dolley Madison are on display in the Madison dining room at Montpelier.

James and Dolley were often surrounded by the huge families of their siblings, and they enlarged Montpelier to accommodate them. Montpelier soon became one of the largest plantations in Orange County and the center of hospitality. At times there were more than 20 children at Montpelier. It was not unusual for them to entertain nearly a hundred for dinner, and 90 guests once came to a Fourth of July picnic. Dolley was so enamored with having guests that when she entertained only 20 or so, she referred to the party as small.

The Madisons also visited relatives all over the county and state. They often dined and partied at different Madison and Taylor homes in the Orange area. They took longer trips to visit Dolley's mother and sisters in Northern Virginia; Madison's sister Nelly Hite's home, Belle Grove, in the Shenandoah Valley; Madison's aunt in Berkeley Springs, West Virginia; and relatives in the James River

valley. They frequently traveled the short drive through the woods to see brother Ambrose's daughter Nelly, who was Madison's favorite niece. Most often, however, they visited sister Sarah and her family.

When Ambrose died, William tried unsuccessfully to assume his role in family councils. He settled on a farm a few miles north of Montpelier. Sarah also settled on a farm near Montpelier, and although Nelly married and moved some distance away, James and Dolley are known to have visited her.

A typical 18th-century kitchen boasts a child's chair from Colonial days.

ONE OF THE GREATEST GRIEFS OF MY LIFE HAS COME TO ME, IN THE PARTING FOR THE FIRST TIME FROM MY SISTER-CHILD.

Dolley Madison

The American Chestnut

Harvested in October, the chestnut is a harbinger of the coming winter season. But its season is short-lived. Available in time for Thanksgiving, fresh chestnuts are gone by January. Their presence, however, provides a touch of nostalgia, and chestnuts roasting by an open fire have become synonymous with the season.

But despite the holiday nostalgia and its presence in songs, the chestnut is virtually unfamiliar to the modern American cook. Before the Civil War and until the early 1900s, chestnuts were plentiful in America. Groves of chestnut trees could be found on many plantations, and the sweet, starchy nut found its way into many Southern dishes. Also a main source of wood, the chestnut tree was popular for building barns, fences, and furniture. However, during the early part of the 20th century, a fungus almost completely eradicated the chestnut tree in this country, and today the American chestnut is extremely rare. Thomas Jefferson planted European chestnuts extensively in Virginia, but they proved to be almost as susceptible to blight as the American species. The chinquapin, a dwarf chestnut native to Virginia and other Southern states, is still plentiful, but it is small and its nutmeat is distinctly different from that of the American chestnut.

Recent years have brought a resurgence in research to develop a blight-resistant chestnut. Connecticut has an extensive collection of American-like chestnuts, and a devoted chestnut grower in Florida is expanding groves of American hybrids. They believe American-grown chestnuts may once again come into our marketplace.

Chestnut burrs and leaves surround a copper bowl of freshly picked chestnuts.

Giblet Gravy

The most important part in making this gravy is to cook the flour in the turkey drippings.

For the giblet broth	1 turkey liver
1 medium onion	Water to cover
1 carrot, peeled and quartered	*For the gravy*
5 sprigs parsley	1/4 cup flour
1 turkey heart, neck,	Turkey drippings
and gizzard	Salt and pepper

Place onion, carrot, parsley, and turkey heart, neck, and gizzard in saucepan. Cover with water and simmer for two hours until gizzard and heart are tender. Add liver and cook an additional 15 minutes. Drain but reserve liquid. Discard onion, carrot, parsley, and turkey neck. Dice heart, gizzard, and livers and set aside. Skim turkey drippings and bring just to boiling point. Lower heat to medium and stir flour slowly into drippings, whisking until smooth. Cook for one minute, stirring constantly. Add giblet broth and whisk briskly to avoid lumps. Cook, stirring constantly, until thick and smooth. Add hot water if mixture is too thick. Add diced giblets and cook for another 2-3 minutes. Salt and pepper to taste.

I AM SADLY DISAP-POINTED AT NOT HAVING MY SISTER LUCY WITH ME . . .
Dolley Madison

Toasted Pecan Wild Rice Dressing

This could supplement or replace the cornbread stuffing or mashed potatoes.

1/2 cup pecans, chopped	1/8 teaspoon cayenne pepper
1 cup wild rice	1/4 teaspoon minced thyme
1 cup long-grain white rice	1 teaspoon salt
4 cups chicken broth	1/4 teaspoon pepper
2 tablespoons butter	

Preheat oven to 350 degrees. Put pecans on cookie sheet in single layer and toast until golden brown, about 3-5 minutes. Combine rice, broth, butter, cayenne, thyme, salt, and pepper. Put in ovenproof bowl and bake until broth is absorbed, about 50 minutes. Add chopped pecans and correct seasoning if necessary. Bake an additional 10 minutes.

Long-Cooked Green Beans

When you cook a country ham, don't throw away the liquor. Use it to cook these beans. They will be delicious.

1-1/2 pounds smoked ham hock
2 quarts cold water
3 pounds whole green beans
Salt and pepper

Place ham hock in large pot and cover with water. Bring to a boil and cook for about one hour. Remove ham hock and add green beans. Simmer for about 30 minutes. Turn off stove and allow beans to sit in water for another 15 to 30 minutes, or until desired ham flavor is reached. Season to taste.

EVERYONE SEEMS TO UNDERCOOK VEGETABLES THESE DAYS, SO THERE ARE MANY PEOPLE WHO HAVE NEVER TASTED BEANS COOKED THIS WAY. I THINK ONE REASON IS THAT THE BEANS ARE SO MUCH MORE TENDER TODAY THAN THEY WERE WHEN I WAS A CHILD.

Edna Lewis

Garlic Mashed Potatoes

Cooking the garlic gives it a much sweeter and less intense flavor than fresh. Its addition to this traditional comfort food raises it to another dimension. If preferred, the garlic can be eliminated.

1 small head garlic
1/2 cup olive oil
8 tablespoons butter
4 pounds russet potatoes

1/2 cup heavy cream
1 tablespoon salt
1 teaspoon white pepper

Peel garlic cloves and sauté in olive oil. Simmer for 10-15 minutes, making sure that garlic does not burn. Strain. Purée garlic cloves with the butter. Set aside. Peel potatoes, cover with salted water and bring to a boil. Cook for about 25 minutes or until tender. Drain. Mix potatoes, using paddle attachment of electric mixer. Add garlic butter, cream, salt, and pepper. Whip until smooth.

Baked Yams and Granny Smith Apples

Just-picked Granny Smith apples sit in a wooden bowl on an antique poplar floor.

As in the early days when ingredients were not measured, our rendition of this popular Southern dish is layered to assure proper distribution of the seasonings.

8 baked yams, cooled
4 Granny Smith apples
4 teaspoons finely chopped
    ginger root
1/8 teaspoon cloves
1/8 teaspoon cardamom

2 teaspoons grated lemon zest
4 teaspoons butter
1/2 cup maple syrup
1/2 cup orange juice
2 tablespoons dark rum

Preheat oven to 375 degrees. Peel and slice yams. Peel and core apples and slice thin. Combine with yams. Mix together ginger root, cloves, cardamom, and lemon zest. Layer the bottom of a baking dish with 1/3 of the yam and apple mixture. Top with 1/3 of the spice mixture. Continue with two more layers. Heat the maple syrup, orange juice, and rum in a small saucepan. Pour over the yams. Bake for about 30 minutes.

Plantation Cornbread

Many different recipes were developed by the colonial women as they attempted to leaven gluten-free cornmeal. This is a rendition of one of them.

1-1/2 cups cornmeal
1 cup flour
1 teaspoon salt
1 teaspoon baking soda
2 cups buttermilk

2 eggs
3 tablespoons vegetable oil
1/3 cup sour cream
1 cup corn kernels

Preheat oven to 450 degrees. Grease a loaf pan. Sift dry ingredients. In separate bowl, beat eggs, buttermilk, oil, and sour cream. Add corn to mixture. Add to dry ingredients and mix until combined. Pour into loaf pan and bake for 25-30 minutes.

*C*ORNBREAD WAS ALWAYS THE LAST THING TO BE MADE WHEN WE PREPARED A MEAL. IT IS JUST SO MUCH BETTER WHEN IT IS HOT AND FRESH FROM THE OVEN.

Edna Lewis

Mincemeat

Mincemeat has filled the winter air with its spicy scent for centuries. The origin of this rich mixture of minced meat, suet, fruit, and spices is obscure; however, it is believed that the marriage between meat and raisins took place during the Crusades, when exotic spices were brought from the East by knights. By the middle of the 1600s, mincemeat had become an integral part of the holiday season. It was thought to bring good luck, and soon it became the custom to eat one pie a day between Christmas and Twelfth Night. Mince pies became very popular in America during the 18th century. A recipe was published in the first cookbook produced in America in 1796.

Mincemeat was made at least a month before Christmas during the butchering season, packed closely in stone crocks, and stored in a cool, dry, dark area to age. A sufficient amount of spices and liquor and ingredients of the highest quality assured the mixture would keep until spring. The meat was boiled until tender and then rubbed through a sieve until it resembled plain gelatin. To this were added chopped apples, currants, raisins, chopped suet, brown sugar, cider, brandy, rum, cloves, nutmeg, and mace.

The adaptability of mincemeat may have been the key to its longevity. Ingredients were varied easily, depending on time and region. Original recipes called for calves' or hogs' feet, but venison became a favorite addition when plentiful; beef and chicken when it was not. Vegetarians eliminated the meat entirely; teetotalers made Temperance pie without any spirits at all.

During the late 19th century, it was discovered that mincemeat could be condensed and packaged, and commercial mincemeat was introduced in 1885. This product, still on the market today, is a boon for modern cooks. But old-fashioned mincemeat is both delicious and easy to make. And the rewards are great.

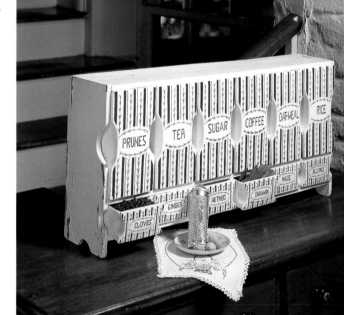

A rare antique cannister set and spice set sits on a 19th-century jelly cupboard.

Traditional Mincemeat

While this recipe is not for the fainthearted, it is considerably simpler than that of colonial days which called for boiling hog feet.

1-1/2 pounds lean beef, cubed
1/2 pound pork suet
4 pounds apples
1 pound dark raisins
1 pound golden raisins
1 pound currants
2/3 cups candied fruit
2 cups brown sugar

1/2 cup molasses
2 teaspoons salt
4 teaspoons ground cinnamon
1/4 teaspoon cloves
1-1/2 teaspoons nutmeg
1-1/2 teaspoons ground mace
3 cups apple cider
2 cups sherry
1 cup brandy

Put beef in medium saucepan, cover with water and boil 1-1/2 hours or until tender. Cool. Using a food processor, chop meat and suet very fine. Combine with apples, raisins, currants, and candied fruit. Place in large saucepan. Add brown sugar, molasses, cider, and spices. Bring to a boil, stirring occasionally. Add sherry and brandy. Simmer 30 minutes. Add more cider if mixture becomes too thick. Let stand 8 hours or longer. Freeze in 2-cup portions in moistureproof containers.

WE ALWAYS MADE OUR OWN HOMEMADE MINCE-MEAT A FEW WEEKS BEFORE CHRISTMAS. IT WAS SO GOOD THAT, ALTHOUGH IT WOULD LAST FROM YEAR TO YEAR, IT WAS ALWAYS GONE BY THE END OF THE WINTER.

Edna Lewis

Fruit Mincemeat

This is a fairly simple filling to make and is far superior to that sold in jars. Be sure to let it age at least 3-4 weeks before using.

1-1/2 pounds chopped pears
1 pound chopped tart apples
3/4 cup dark raisins
3/4 cup golden raisins
3/4 cup currants
3/4 cup dried figs, chopped
3/4 cup dried apricots, chopped
1 tablespoon candied ginger
1/2 cup slivered almonds

1/2 teaspoon cinnamon
1/4 teaspoon mace
1/4 teaspoon nutmeg
1/4 teaspoon cloves
1/8 teaspoon ginger
1 tablespoon lemon peel, grated
1/3 cup lemon juice
1 cup apple cider
1/2 cup brandy

Combine all ingredients except brandy in a large saucepan and bring to a boil. Cook for 10 minutes. Remove from heat. Add brandy and let stand 8 hours or longer. Add additional cider if mixture gets too thick. Store at room temperature.

Caramel-Pumpkin Custard

This lighter version of pumpkin pie is a welcome treat after a heavy Thanksgiving meal.

For the caramel
1-1/2 cups granulated sugar
1 teaspoon lemon juice
1/4 cup water

In a small saucepan, combine sugar, lemon juice, and water. Cook until caramelized and dark amber in color. If sugar crystals form, carefully remove from sides of pan with a pastry brush that has been dipped in water.

For the custard
1 cup cooked pumpkin
2 cups granulated sugar
5 eggs
4 egg yolks
2 cups half-and-half

2 cups evaporated milk
1 teaspoon vanilla extract
1/4 teaspoon allspice
1/4 teaspoon ginger
1/2 teaspoon cinnamon

Preheat oven to 350 degrees. Coat a 9-1/2-inch springform pan with caramel. Purée pumpkin. Combine all ingredients. Strain through fine sieve. Pour into springform pan and place in a large pan filled with 1 inch of water. Bake for 1-1/2 hours or until knife inserted one inch from center comes out clean. Refrigerate at least 8 hours. Before serving invert and unmold onto serving platter.

A portrait of Erasmus Taylor, the great uncle of Presidents James Madison and Zachary Taylor, hangs above a 1790 mantel.

Hot toddies and chestnuts are served on an 18th-century tilt-top table.

Hot Toddies

Hot toddies can also be made with brandy or any whiskey but the bourbon makes them pure Virginia.

8 lumps of sugar
32 ounces boiling water
16 ounces brandy
Lemon slices
Nutmeg

Place a lump of sugar in the bottom of each mug. Add 4 ounces water and 2 ounces brandy. Garnish with lemon slice. Grate nutmeg on top.

WHEN I WAS A CHILD, I NEVER SAW A BOTTLE OF BOURBON. THE ADULTS WOULD FILL THEIR GLASSES IN THE KITCHEN AND BRING THEM TO THE TABLE. THE BOTTLE WAS NEVER IN SIGHT. THE AROMA WAS VERY DISTINCT, HOWEVER, AND I CAME TO ASSOCIATE BOURBON WITH SPECIAL OCCASIONS.

Edna Lewis

Winter

Winter in Piedmont Virginia is a time for romance. The rolling hills become a canvas of white punctuated with brilliant red cardinals. Tree branches drip with ice shimmering like diamonds in the sun. Thousands of stars dot a crystal-clear sky. It is a perfect time to snuggle up by the fire and enjoy quiet conversation.

With the harvest over and spring planting months away, Virginians used the winter months as a time to rest. And a time to party. Families and friends gathered to celebrate the holidays. Feasts, foxhunts, music, dancing, songs, and games were the order of the day. And it was a favorite time for weddings.

In an effort to dispel the bleakness of a winter day, fresh-smelling evergreens were brought inside as a reminder that spring was not far away. Mantels, railings, and windows held fresh wreaths and garlands. Fresh-cut greenery was arranged in vases. Dried herbs and flowers were scattered about.

As in other seasons, hospitality and friendship were the hallmark of the plantation. Warm fires blazed. Food and drink were offered in abundance. Merrymaking continued nonstop. And when news of Virginia's generosity to family, friends, and even strangers reached England, the term "Southern Hospitality" was born.

*G*ame brought another kind of meat into the larder. Hunting was not considered a sport then, but rather a way to add variety to the food supply and make the meals more interesting. The catch would be drawn and then left to hang in the fur. It was then prepared and exchanged with neighbors during the Christmas season, along with the fruits that had been canned in the fall.

Christmas was a time of enjoying special foods. We began with a huge breakfast of sausages, eggs, fresh biscuits with preserves, along with crispy fried oysters. The men indulged with special coffee mixed with cocoa and bourbon that we children, of course, were not allowed to taste. Christmas dinner was a long affair with us all sitting around for hours enjoying all the good things Mother had been up half the night preparing. We then spent Christmas week visiting the neighbors and enjoying their baked goods and the wines they had prepared from dandelions, elderberries, wild plums, and grapes.

The last important job of winter was cutting the ice. During the coldest part of January, the men would head out to the frozen rivers and ponds. We often bundled up and followed them, as we loved to watch them cut up the ice and then haul the huge blocks back to the ice house. The ice house was a deep cellar lined with poles. The men would lower the ice down into the cellar and then surround it with straw to help keep it frozen until summer. We watched with excitement as the trap door was closed. Then we went home to wait for spring and dream of the summer when we would pull out the ice to make our homemade ice cream and iced tea.

Edna Lewis

A Feast for the Holidays

Early in December, the plantation takes on a festive look. Grand old holly trees and nandina bushes are bursting with bright red berries. Mantels and stairwells overflow with magnolia, pine, and cedar. Windows are filled with wreaths made from boxwood and yew. Osage oranges, yarrow, and cones from pine and cedar trees adorn the wreaths.

Anchored by an unbelievable collection of Madison treasures, Meadowfarm is decorated to illustrate the Yuletide in 19th-century Virginia. Every room in the manor house is decorated with a profusion of freshly cut greens.

The dining room awaits a gathering of family and friends. The menu reflects a Christmas feast typical of the Old Dominion: succulent oysters fresh from the Chesapeake Bay, thick slices of juicy venison, cakes redolent of sharp spices and crystallized fruits, steaming mincemeat rich with mellow spirits, and a quaff of wassail not for the fainthearted. When the halls are decked, presents arrayed, and fires lighted, a holiday dinner is the perfect way to share time with people you know well and those you would like to know better.

Chippendale chairs surround a walnut table set for a holiday dinner in a dining room that contains an arm chair and tall-case clock that belonged to James and Dolley Madison.

Meadowfarm

A long driveway, winding through an avenue of red and silver maples, leads to Meadowfarm, which has been in the possession of one family for more than 275 years. The ancestral home of James Madison's cousin, Zachary Taylor, Meadowfarm is currently owned by an eighth-generation descendant of James Taylor II.

The earliest house was built in 1727 by the elder Zachary Taylor and his wife, Elizabeth Lee. In 1858, it was replaced with the present house, which stands in a beautiful park of 25 acres immediately in front of the original homestead. The crisp, elegant proportions of this beautiful white-painted brick house make it one of the finest examples of Greek Revival style in the region.

The gardens, designed by Charles Gillette, surround the spring house, bath house, and guest quarters of antebellum heritage. An ancient black walnut of massive proportions, probably the oldest tree on the plantation, stands at the entrance. Always a master, Gillette created an enchanting fountain that ripples over a rocky rill and spills into a fish pond bordered with swamp laurel, magnolias, weeping cherries, beeches, and willow plumbago.

A large reception hall with a spectacular stairway presents a breathtaking entrance to the house. Black marble mantels set off a large double parlor on its north side. To the south side are two smaller rooms with identical woodwork and mantels. All these rooms contain significant heirlooms and artifacts belonging to both the Madison and Taylor families. A cherished memory of the Taylors is an autographed photograph of Robert E. Lee, a frequent visitor when he was encamped nearby during the Civil War. Given to the Taylor family in appreciation of this hospitality, the photograph is lovingly displayed in the parlor.

A Holiday Feast

Menu

Chesapeake Oyster Stew

Roasted Goose with Applejack and Winter Fruits

Loin of Fallow Fields Venison

Sweet Potato Gratin

Braised Red Cabbage

Persimmon, Orange, and Chestnut Chutney

Black Currant Bread Pudding

Dark Chocolate Cheesecake with Cranberry Coulis

Light Fruitcake

Wassail

Wassail

Popular in Virginia since colonial days, Wassail will float heavenly aromas throughout the house.

1 quart boiling water	1/4 teaspoon powdered ginger
1 quart ale or red wine	3 eggs
1 lemon, peel only	1/2 cup sugar
1/4 teaspoon grated nutmeg	1 quart rum or brandy

Put a metal spoon into punch bowl and each of two pitchers. Add boiling water down the spoons, swirl around and let stand. Heat ale to boiling point, but do not boil. Add lemon peel, nutmeg, and ginger. Beat together eggs and sugar. Discard water from each pitcher. In one pitcher combine egg mixture and hot wine or ale. Pour rum or brandy into the second pitcher. Pour mixtures back and forth from one pitcher to another until smooth. Discard water from punch bowl and fill with wassail. Serve hot.

Wassail is served in a vintage pressed glass punch bowl.

WHEN OYSTERS ARRIVED AT OUR COUNTRY STORE, MY MOTHER WOULD SEND US OFF TO BUY SOME FOR OUR HOLIDAY DINNERS. SHE ALWAYS GAVE US SMALL BUCKETS TO FILL WITH THE OYSTERS. THEN SHE WOULD PREPARE THEM FRIED, SCALLOPED, IN STUFFING, AND IN STEWS.

Edna Lewis

Oyster Stew

Once you add the oysters, heat just to a boil. Do not boil or the cream will curdle.

2 pints oysters with liquid	1/4 teaspoon salt
10 tablespoons butter	1/4 teaspoon black pepper
1-1/2 cups milk	Dash of cayenne pepper
2-1/2 cups heavy cream	

Melt 2 tablespoons of butter in saucepan. Add undrained oysters and cook over medium heat, stirring constantly, until oyster edges curl. In another saucepan, scald milk and cream. Add oysters and bring just to boiling point, stirring constantly. Season to taste. Heat large serving bowl or soup tureen and put 8 tablespoons butter in bottom. Ladle soup into hot bowl or tureen.

Holiday Traditions

In antebellum days, preparation for the holiday season got off to an early start. Smoke from every farm in early November signaled that it was hog butchering time. No planter would have imagined a holiday without huge cured and smoked hams, sausage, souse, and pig's foot jelly. Once hog killing was out of the way, the men began cutting, hauling, and stacking wood. Inside the house, things were just as active. Big fruitcakes and plum puddings were baked, smothered with home-made wine, wrapped in cloth and stored to ripen. And all kinds of cakes, pies, breads, and cookies were baked every day until all the shelves were filled.

The week before Christmas began a round of gaiety that lasted through the new year. It was a time of relaxation from work and worry. Everyone came home. It was a merry crowd. There was a party every night, and everyone went to every party. They played games and danced. The cellar was stocked well, so there was no cooking to be done. But buffet tables still groaned. Highlights were pungent holiday desserts and beautifully arranged towers of luscious fruit.

A newell post is decorated with natural greens found around the plantation.

I AM LESS WORRIED HERE WITH AN HUNDRED VISITORS THAN WITH TWENTY-FIVE IN WASHINGTON.

Dolley Madison

The holiday table is set with Limoges china that belonged to President Zachary Taylor.

Loin of Fallow Fields Venison

Venison should be served medium rare. It is very lean and gets dry if overcooked.

2 carrots
1/2 large onion
1 shallot
1 large clove garlic
1 tablespoon olive oil
2-1/2 cups red wine

1/4 cup red wine vinegar
2 bay leaves
1 teaspoon sea salt
6 black peppercorns
5-lb loin of venison

Peel and chop carrots, onion, shallot, and garlic. Combine with remaining ingredients. Cover venison with marinade. Refrigerate for at least 8 hours. Remove from refrigerator and discard marinade. Roast venison in 350-degree oven for about 2-1/2 hours or until meat thermometer registers 120 degrees.

CHRISTMAS WAS A SPECIAL TIME IN OUR KITCHEN. WE SPENT DAYS PREPARING FOODS THAT WE DIDN'T HAVE ANY OTHER TIME OF THE YEAR.

Edna Lewis

Braised Red Cabbage

This dish will taste even better if prepared a day ahead. Be sure to store it in a container that is not aluminum or it will turn color.

1 head red cabbage
1 onion
2 tart apples
3 tablespoons olive oil
1/3 cup sugar

1 cup chicken stock
1/2 cup red wine
1 cup red wine vinegar
Salt and pepper

Core cabbage and cut into thin strips. Peel and dice onion and apples and slowly sauté in olive oil. Add sugar and liquid ingredients, cover and cook for about 10 minutes, until cabbage is tender. Season to taste.

The foyer at Willow Grove is appointed with 18th-century tables and original portraits of Virginia gentry.

Roasted Goose with Applejack and Winter Fruits

The sweetness of the fruit paired with the richness of the goose make this an outstanding dish to take the place of honor on a holiday table.

1 goose, 6 to 8 pounds
Oil for sautéing
3 large russet potatoes
1-1/2 cups pitted prunes
1/2 cup dried apricots
2 cups apple brandy
3 cooking apples
3/4 cup celery, diced
3/4 cup onion, diced
4 cups dry bread, cubed

2 tablespoons fresh thyme
2 tablespoons minced sage
1/4 cup fresh minced parsley
3/4 cup walnuts, chopped
8 slices crisp bacon, crumbled
1/2 teaspoon ginger
3/4 cup poultry stock
Salt and pepper
Nutmeg

A perfectly cooked goose waits to be served on antique Picard porcelain plates.

For the stuffing
Put prunes, apricots, and brandy in a saucepan. Bring to boil and remove from heat. Let soak at least 8 hours. Drain and reserve liquid. Peel potatoes and cut into cubes. Toss with oil and roast in 425-degree oven until browned and crisp, about 20 minutes. Peel apples and cut into small pieces. Sauté apples, celery, and onions until onions are translucent. Combine bread, potatoes, onions, celery, fruits, thyme, sage, parsley, nuts, and bacon. Pour hot stock over mixture and mix lightly. Season to taste with salt, pepper, and nutmeg.

For the goose
Remove giblets and neck from goose. Discard liver. Put giblets and neck in a saucepan. Cover with water and cook for about 2 hours to make a stock. Set aside. Rinse goose with cold water and pat dry. Prick fatty areas of goose with exception of the breast. Rub with salt, pepper, and ginger. Stuff cavity with fruit mixture and close by sewing or using skewers. Place on rack in roasting pan. Roast uncovered at 400 degrees for 30 minutes. Reduce heat to 325 degrees and roast, basting with pan juices, for an additional 2 to 2-1/2 hours until juices run clear. Remove goose from pan and skim off fat. Deglaze pan with reserved apple brandy. Remove stuffing from goose. Place goose on platter and surround with fruit stuffing. Pour pan sauce over goose.

The Christmas Tree

No one is completely sure how the custom of the Christmas tree began. It has been said that it may have descended from the Tree of Life as it was portrayed in many medieval plays about Adam and Eve. And it has also been said it may have come about from pagan winter festivals where evergreens were used in fertility rites. But it is generally agreed that the Christmas tree was first introduced to America by the Germans.

The first actual record of decorated trees appeared in 1520 in Alsace, and by the early 1600s, the tradition of a Christmas tree was firmly established in Germany. German-born Moravians decorated trees in their homes when they settled in Pennsylvania during the mid-18th century. Hessian soldiers decorated a tree at Christmas during the Revolutionary War. And it was German-born Charles Minnegerode, a professor of classic languages at the College of William and Mary, who started the custom in Virginia that continued throughout the South.

Minnegerode, one of a large, affectionate family, had a special fondness for children.

He was often invited to the homes of his colleagues where he told the children stories of the events of olden days, among them several about the Christmas tree.

As Christmas approached in 1842, Minnegerode felt homesick for his native Germany. He thus planned a holiday party for the children in much the same manner he knew his relatives in Germany would be enjoying. As he had always done at home, he rode out to the woods where he cut a fresh tree and placed it in the parlor. But he had no shiny glass globes, no tinsel garland to adorn the tree. So he formed popcorn globes, strung cranberries for garland, and gilded nuts for brightness.

The custom started to take hold, and by the mid-1800s, trees were being decorated throughout the South. The popularity of the Christmas tree increased in 1848 when a London newspaper printed a portrait of Queen Victoria and her family grouped around a twinkling fir tree.

As the century progressed, the fashion of decorating trees spread. And a tradition began.

Heirloom toys decorate and surround a large tree.

Sweet Potato Gratin

This is a delicious modification of old-fashioned scalloped potatoes.

6 sweet potatoes
5 Idaho potatoes
6 egg yolks
1 quart heavy cream
1 teaspoon grated nutmeg
Salt and pepper

Preheat oven to 350 degrees. Lightly butter a 6 x 9 baking dish. Peel white and sweet potatoes. Slice very thin. Set aside. Beat egg yolks and cream together. Alternate layers of sweet potatoes, white potatoes, and cream mixture, seasoning each layer with salt and pepper. Press down gently. Cover with aluminum foil and bake for 2-1/2 hours. Remove foil and brown in oven a few minutes.

More than a thousand antique German ornaments and real candles make this tree a spectacular sight.

Persimmon, Orange, and Chestnut Chutney

Persimmons have the best flavor after a frost, so Christmas is the perfect time to enjoy this delicious chutney.

1 pomegranate
10 roasted chestnuts
4 large navel oranges
1 persimmon

1/2 cup chopped red onion
3 teaspoons virgin olive oil
1/4 cup balsamic vinegar

Cut pomegranate into quarters with a sharp knife. Separate seeds. Peel chestnuts and chop coarsely. Slice ends off each orange. Set each orange securely on counter and slice away the peel, using downward sawing motion. Slice peeled oranges into thin rounds and place in shallow bowl. Remove stem, peel, and cube persimmon. Toss with peeled oranges. Scatter onions, pomegranate seeds, and chopped chestnuts over orange-persimmon mixture. Dribble oil and balsamic vinegar over surface.

A TYPICAL DINNER ON CHRISTMAS EVE USUALLY INCLUDED A POTATO GRATIN, OR SCALLOPED POTATOES AS WE CALLED THEM THEN. WE USED WHITE POTATOES LAYERED WITH BOUILLON AND BUTTER.

Edna Lewis

Saving the Treasures

As the War of 1812 escalated in August of 1814, British troops headed to Washington. President Madison left the President's Mansion to be with the soldiers in the Washington suburb of Bladensburg, Maryland. The city of Washington was in turmoil. Dolley remained, ever fearful of what might confront the President. She received a letter from him urging her to pack up and flee the city immediately. But Dolley was determined not to leave until he returned unharmed to accompany her.

Dolley waited anxiously for the next two days, cramming the Declaration of Independence, the Constitution, and other government papers into four large crates and watching as hordes of people fled the city. Once she felt the government papers were secure, Dolley looked around at her personal belongings and realized that she couldn't leave them, even though there was little space in which to pack them. She did succeed, however, in packing some of her clothing, the silverware, a favorite clock, and even the crimson draperies. She then had her staff prepare dinner for her husband and his officers to enjoy when they returned.

Dolley managed to secure a wagon and get everything stowed securely. However, one item that she dearly loved still remained—the Gilbert Stuart portrait of George Washington, which was screwed to the wall. The enemy was so close that she could hear the cannons, but she refused to leave without the portrait. Unscrewing the portrait from the wall would have taken too long at such a perilous time, so Dolley ordered the frame broken and the canvas removed. She then got in the loaded carriage and fled to Alexandria. Folklore has it that she was dressed unconventionally so that she wouldn't be noticed by the British.

Unfortnately, James and his officers never returned to enjoy the meal that was prepared for them. But the invading British soldiers, seeing the table ready for a sumptuous meal, sat down and gorged themselves.

James and Dolley met again in Alexandria. They returned to Washington, appalled at the sight of the Capital City. Fire had destroyed the Mansion. And what the flames hadn't destroyed, the British did. They had smashed some of the furniture and burned the rest, leaving it in piles of ashes.

Disheartened, but undaunted, she worked tirelessly to bring the social graces back to Washington, entertaining as skillfully and graciously as ever.

Golden angels are handmade of papier maché.

Dark Chocolate Cheesecake with Cranberry Coulis

The slight tang of the cranberries adds a different dimension to this decadent cheesecake.

For the chocolate crumb crust
1/2 package Oreo cookies
1/4 cup butter, softened

For the filling
1/2 pound semisweet
    chocolate
1-1/2 pounds cream cheese
2 eggs
1 cup sugar
2 tablespoons heavy cream
1 tablespoon Kahlua
1 tablespoon dark rum
3/4 cup sour cream

A chocolate cheesecake sitting on a gold Picard plate makes a festive Christmas dessert.

Preheat oven to 350 degrees. In a food processor combine Oreos and butter to form a crumb mixture. Press mixture onto the bottom and sides of a 12-inch springform pan. In a double boiler, melt chocolate. Keep warm. Beat the cream cheese until smooth. Add the remaining ingredients except the chocolate. Beat until smooth. Add the chocolate. Beat until chocolate is incorporated. Pour mixture into the crust and wrap the outside of the pan with foil to make it watertight. Place springform pan in larger pan that contains 1/2-inch water. Put in oven and turn down to 300 degrees. After 15 minutes, reduce oven to 275 degrees. Bake for 1-1/2 hours or until a straw comes out clean. Remove from water bath and remove foil from the pan. Let cool on rack.

Cranberry Coulis

2 cups fresh cranberries
1/2 cup sugar
1/2 cup water

Place cranberries, sugar, and water in saucepan. Bring to a boil and cook for about 10 minutes. Purée mixture in food processor until smooth. Strain.

I HAVE PRESSED AS MANY CABINET PAPERS INTO TRUNKS AS TO FILL ONE CARRIAGE.

Dolley Madison

Vintage Christmas ornaments include handmade 19th-century houses.

Vintage Ornaments

Ornaments for Christmas trees have always been special, and those saved over the years become even more so. Wonderful little handmade dolls and ornate silver candle holders on tree clips all went to mix with blown glass balls and hand-strung garlands for individual trees.

In plantation manor homes, tall ceilings allowed 12- to 14-foot trees cut from nearby woods for family members and friends to help decorate. By the late 19th century, when decoration in American homes reached its zenith, trees were covered with bits of lace, mercury glass balls, paper diecuts, crystal icicles, wax angels of all sizes, and thousands of beads, baubles, and garlands.

Light Fruitcake

There is no citron in this recipe so even those not fond of fruitcake find it delicious.

1 pound pitted dates	1 cup butter
1 pound light raisins	3 eggs, beaten
2 pounds candied cherries	3 cups applesauce
1 pound candied pineapple	5 cups flour
1 pound chopped Brazil nuts	1/2 teaspoon cinnamon
1 pound chopped walnuts	1/2 teaspoon ground nutmeg
1/4 cup bourbon whiskey	1/2 teaspoon ground cloves
2 cups sugar	4 teaspoons baking soda

Preheat oven to 275 degrees. Butter a large loaf pan and line with buttered parchment or brown paper. Mix together dates, raisins, cherries, pineapple, and nuts. Pour bourbon over mixture. Toss with 1 cup flour and set aside. Cream sugar and butter until light and fluffy. Add eggs and applesauce and mix well. Sift together remaining flour, baking soda, cinnamon, nutmeg, and cloves. Add to butter mixture and mix well. Fold in fruit and nut mixture. Bake for 2 hours.

Black Currant Bread Pudding

The sabayon is an updated version of the custard that was usually passed with bread pudding in earlier times.

10 slices white bread
1/2 cup black currants
4 tablespoons butter, melted
5 eggs, beaten

1/2 cup sugar
1 tablespoon kirschwasser
2 cups half-and-half
1 teaspoon vanilla extract

Allow white bread to dry out. Preheat oven to 350 degrees. Butter a large loaf pan. Trim crusts off and cut bread into 1/2-inch cubes. Combine bread and currants in a large bowl. Pour melted butter over bread and currants and set aside. Whisk together eggs, sugar, and liquor. Scald half-and-half. Slowly whisk into egg mixture. Cool, strain, and pour over cubed bread. Press bread and currant mixture into prepared loaf pan. Pour remaining custard in bowl over bread mixture, being careful not to fill pan more than 1/2-inch from the top. Place loaf pan in shallow baking pan filled with 1 inch of water. Bake 55-60 minutes or until a knife inserted 1 inch from the center comes out clean. Let pudding cool in loaf pan until warm to the touch. Run a butter knife around sides of loaf pan and turn pudding out into a serving dish. Slice and serve with Southern Comfort sabayon.

For the sabayon
6 egg yolks
1/4 cup sugar
1/4 cup Southern Comfort
1 teaspoon vanilla
1 teaspoon allspice

Combine egg yolks, sugar, Southern Comfort, vanilla, and allspice in a mixing bowl and whip together. Place bowl over simmering water, whipping the mixture constantly until it becomes thick and fluffy.

WE ALWAYS HAD BREAD PUDDING IN THE SPRING WHEN NEW CALVES PRODUCED EXTRA MILK. I CAN STILL REMEMBER THE RICH SMELL OF BUTTER AND NUTMEG RISING FROM THE PUDDING AS IT COOLED ON THE KITCHEN TABLE.

Edna Lewis

During the holidays, poinsettias adorn each table in Clark's Tavern at Willow Grove.

Greenery

Evergreens, regarded as symbols of life through the cold winter days, were used as decorations in pagan festivals. Romans used greenery to celebrate the renewal of life at the new year. They decked their homes with holly and ivy and gave sprigs of them to friends as good luck tokens during their midwinter feast. As Christianity took hold, religious symbolism was given to both holly and ivy.

Mistletoe, however, gained no religious recognition. Believed to have been hung over the doors of the British Isle Druids to protect them against witchcraft, mistletoe was shunned by the church. Thus it has never been included in church decorations and has never been written about in a Christmas hymn. But, however negatively the church might have thought of mistletoe, no

The Madison dining room fireplace at Montpelier is decorated in greenery gathered from the plantation.

Christmas in the 19th century was complete without it; any maiden who escaped being kissed under the mistletoe knew she would not marry within the year.

Virginians decorated their homes and churches with a wide variety of greenery, and collecting the large amounts necessary was an arduous task. Holly, ivy, magnolia, pine, boxwood, laurel, bay, and yew were combined to bring in the fresh aroma of the forest and provide a sense of being in touch with nature. To avoid monotony, different shades of green were combined. Holly was especially popular because it bore red fruit when nothing else had color. And dried apples and dried flowers were often added to perk up the evergreen decorations.

A Brunch for the New Year

At the beginning of the new year, when the days are cold, the panes frosty, and the hills covered with a soft white snow, the aura of days long past is particularly emphasized. Much the same as in those days, a warm welcome and a roaring fire are perfect antidotes to a cold wintry day.

New Year's celebrations were very different on the plantation. Instead of a night of partying, New Year's Eve was more of a family gathering, a time to take down the Christmas tree, reflect on the past year, and prepare for the guests who would be arriving the next morning. New Year's Day often began with holiday sportsmen off before dawn to partake in one of Virginia's favorite holiday occupations—the hunt. After a hearty breakfast, the gentlemen then spent the rest of the day fulfilling social

A feather topiary makes an interesting centerpiece for a holiday brunch.

duties by calling on ladies and feasting and quaffing brandy-spiked eggnog.

The night often ended with a ceremonial burning of the Christmas tree as many planters believed the tree should stand no longer than New Year's Day.

Here we celebrate the New Year with a sumptuous brunch. The dining room, furnished with 18th- and 19th-

century antiques, is a magnificent setting. Fireplaces are ablaze and soft music fills the air.

As in days past, the table is set with beautiful china and crystal. Food and spirits are plentiful. And, in true Virginia tradition, the menu includes pork and blackeyed peas to ensure good luck for the coming year.

Greenwood

Overlooking blooming shrubs and a lovely garden, Greenwood provides the serene atmosphere reminiscent of antebellum Virginia.

Greenwood was built as a summer home by John Baylor, a wealthy planter and landowner in the Virginia Tidewater. Typical of most influential men of his time, Baylor was a friend of George Washington and a neighbor of James Madison, Sr., father of the President. Madison was building Montpelier about the same time Baylor was building Greenwood. Their designs were quite similar, and it could be assumed both men shared the same builders.

Thomas Macon and his wife, Sarah Madison Macon, sister of the President, purchased the Greenwood house and adjoining acres from Baylor. They subsequently conveyed the property to their daughter, Lucy Conway, who named the estate Greenwood. Lucy and her husband Reuben were childless, so upon her death, the property was conveyed to her nieces and nephews. It remained in the family until 1900.

The oldest portion of the house, a two-story frame section set on a brick cellar with brick end chimneys, dates to the second half of the 18th century. The Federal style of the mantels and wainscoting points to the possibility of an early remodeling, probably by the Macons or the Conways. A story-and-a-half wing, added some years after the two-story section was completed, has undergone many changes. Except for a Greek Revival style mantel of mid-19th century vintage, few old features survive. The house is furnished with antiques and family heirlooms.

Although Greenwood was not an elegant and prestigious home, it has been a survivor of its time and style—a simple summer residence of one of Virginia's colonial leaders and the home of the niece of one of our nation's founding fathers. Socially prominent in the mid-1800s, Greenwood fell into disrepair until the mid-1930s when it was modernized.

A Brunch for the New Year

Menu

Dolley Madison's Bouillon

Sautéed Sweetbreads with Chestnuts

Country-Fried Virginia Apples

Spicy Sausage Gravy over Stone-Ground Corn Muffins

Philadelphia Scrapple

Smoked Chicken Hash

Iron Skillet Country Omelet

Turnip Hash Browns

Blackeyed Peas with Ham Hocks

Cinnamon-Orange French Toast with Burnt Orange Syrup

Assorted Muffins

Old-Fashioned Tea Biscuits

Holiday Eggnog

Dolley's Bouillon

This old Virginia recipe is probably close to that used to prepare the bouillon Dolley offered her guests when they first arrived at Montpelier.

I REMEMBER MY MOTHER PACKING THERMOS BOTTLES OF HOT BOUILLON WHEN WE WENT TO THE MONTPELIER RACES IN THE FALL. IT TOOK THE CHILL OUT OF THE NOVEMBER AIR AND SEEMED TO GIVE US AN APPETITE TO ENJOY THE HUGE PICNIC SHE ALWAYS PREPARED.

Edna Lewis

5 pounds bone-in chuck roast
2 pounds beef bones
3 quarts water
1 large onion
6 cloves
2 carrots
1 leek

1 bunch celery
6 peppercorns
1 bay leaf
1 small bunch parsley
1/2 teaspoon fresh thyme
1 tablespoon salt

Place beef and bones in pot containing cold water. Bring to scalding and reduce to slow simmer. Do not let it boil. As the gray scum forms, skim off and discard. Continue until the broth is clear. Add the rest of the ingredients. Cover loosely and simmer for about 6 hours. Remove from burner and strain. Set aside to cool. When cool, skim off all fat. Broth should be perfectly clear.

Holiday Eggnog

It is very important to stir the liquor into the eggs so they cook.

12 eggs, separated
1 cup sugar
1 quart half-and-half
1 quart vanilla ice cream

1 fifth brandy
1 fifth rum
1 teaspoon nutmeg

Beat egg yolks with sugar until thick and light yellow. Add rum and brandy and mix well. Add half-and-half and mix well. Add ice cream and stir until melted. Beat egg whites until stiff. Spoon egg whites onto mixture and dust with nutmeg.

Sautéed Sweetbreads with Chestnuts

Traditionally, sweetbreads were combined with oysters to make a pie during the holidays. Colonial cookbooks tout it as the most delicious pie that could be made, with the veal sweetbreads the most delicious ingredient.

2-1/2 pounds veal sweetbreads
1 bay leaf
2 stalks celery, minced
2 carrots, sliced
2 shallots, chopped
1/4 cup country ham, chopped

Pinch of cardamom
Pepper to taste
1 cup rich chicken stock
1/2 pound boiled chestnuts
1/4 cup port
2 tablespoons butter

Put sweetbreads in pan and cover with water. Add bay leaf and poach for 5 minutes. Allow sweetbreads to cool in the broth for 10 minutes and then peel carefully, pulling away the thin membrane and all the little tubes and bits of fat. Put them in a shallow pan, weight them down with a flat pan, and refrigerate for 2 hours. Remove sweetbreads from refrigerator. Sauté celery with leaves, carrot, shallots, and ham in one tablespoon butter. Add cardamom, pepper, and sweetbreads to mixture. Add chicken stock. Braise for about 10 minutes. Remove sweetbreads from mixture and slice. Mix with whole chestnuts and flambé with port. Strain resulting sauce, reduce, and add one tablespoon butter. Pour sauce over sweetbread and chestnut mixture and heat through. Put in a baking dish and glaze in a 500-degree oven.

WE HAD PORK RATHER THAN VEAL SWEETBREADS SINCE THEY WERE ALWAYS AVAILABLE AND PLENTIFUL RIGHT AFTER HOG BUTCHERING. AFTER WE PARBOILED THEM, WE SLICED THEM, DIPPED THEM IN EGG, AND DREDGED THEM IN FLOUR. THEN WE FRIED THE SLICES UNTIL THEY WERE CRISP.

Edna Lewis

Country-Fried Virginia Apples

No Southern Sunday breakfast was complete without this dish.

8 apples, peeled and cored
4 tablespoons bacon fat
2/3 cup sugar
Pinch of nutmeg

Cut apples into quarters. Then cut each quarter in half. Heat bacon fat in hot skillet. When fat is sizzling, add apples. Cover and cook briskly until apples are soft. Remove cover and sprinkle apples with sugar and nutmeg. Cook, stirring frequently, until apples begin to brown.

Dolley's Table

Dining tables in the 18th century adhered to very strict visual requirements. Tables were set in true Georgian style with symmetry the rule of the day. Every platter was balanced with a similar one. The table was fully set before guests arrived. And guests left the room after each course so the table could be cleared.

Candlesticks were used only when the darkness of the night made them necessary. A huge platter of meat or pyramid of sweets took stage as the centerpiece. In some instances, wealthy hostesses had centerpieces of miniature landscapes created from sugar, pastry, and marzipan.

One can easily imagine how beautifully Dolley would have decorated her table. A skillful hostess with old-fashioned elegance, she cut no corners in her effort to bring happiness and comfort to those around her. She offered only the finest foods and wines served on the finest imported French porcelain.

Dolley began buying French porcelain shortly after her marriage to James in 1794.

She eventually acquired four complete sets which she used for dining and for tea. In addition, she also had a set of "Canton" porcelain, named after a region in China.

Remaining today are cups and saucers given to her by James Monroe when he was in France negotiating the Louisiana Purchase. It is easy to visualize this beautiful china, with its hand-painted gilt borders, set atop her jacquard weave linen damask tablecloth. Most likely designed specifically for Dolley's dining table, the 17-foot long imported French cloth had a fall pattern of pheasants, pumpkins, and pineapples. This table would

have probably been the focal point of many feasts at Montpelier.

Once guests had left the dining room, decanters of wine and silverplated baskets laden with sweetmeats and confections would have been laid upon her gleaming mahogany dining table. If the season allowed, Dolley was sure to have had a bouquet of flowers set in an urn on the table. For a winter feast, however, she may likely have turned to silk or sugared flower petals to garnish her table. A true 18th-century country woman, Dolley would have ended the evening by dipping tobacco from her silver snuffbox.

A traditional Williamsburg curve centers a table set with an antique gold and white damask cloth and monogrammed Limoges porcelain.

Spicy Sausage Gravy

A combination of Italian sausage with chorizo or andouille can be used in place of the homemade sausage.

For the sausage
3/4 pound lean pork
1/4 pound pork fat
3 tablespoons minced sage
2 teaspoons minced thyme

1 garlic clove, chopped
1 teaspoon crushed red pepper
1 teaspoon cayenne pepper
1 teaspoon black pepper
1 teaspoon salt

Put meat through fine blade of grinder twice. Assemble rest of ingredients. Add to meat and mix well. Correct seasoning. Roll into cylinder and wrap in plastic. Refrigerate for at least 24 hours.

For the gravy
10 ounces country-style sausage
1 teaspoon cumin
1 teaspoon cayenne pepper
1 teaspoon ground sage

1 teaspoon thyme
1 teaspoon paprika
1 cup heavy cream
Salt and pepper

Break sausage into small pieces and sauté in hot skillet until brown. Season with cumin, cayenne, sage, thyme, and paprika. Add heavy cream and simmer until thickened. Season with salt and pepper.

Yes, HE SPENT NEARLY THREE WEEKS WITH US, OFF AND ON, AND SEEMED TO ENJOY HIMSELF VERY MUCH.

Dolley Madison

Stone-Ground Corn Muffins

These muffins are feather light if the sour cream and baking soda mixture rests about 15 minutes.

1 teaspoon baking soda
2 cups sour cream
2 eggs, beaten
2-1/2 cups all-purpose flour

1-1/2 cups yellow cornmeal
6 teaspoons baking powder
1 teaspoon salt
1/2 cup sugar

Preheat oven to 350 degrees. Combine baking soda and sour cream and stir until frothy. Add eggs, whisk, and set aside. In separate bowl, sift together flour, cornmeal, baking powder, salt, and sugar. Combine the two mixtures and mix just until blended. Drop by teaspoonfuls into greased mini-muffin pans. Bake about 15-20 minutes.

Philadelphia Scrapple

From a very old recipe which we have updated, this scrapple is best when fried to form a crisp outside crust.

4-1/2 pounds pork ribs	1-1/2 pounds pork liver
1 bay leaf	5 cups water
2 teaspoons chopped thyme	1-1/2 cups cornmeal
2 onions, diced	Salt and pepper

Simmer pork ribs with the salt, bay leaf, thyme, and 1 onion until the meat falls off the bones. Remove meat and set liquor to cool. Remove bones and gristle and chop the meat fine. Grind pork liver and 1 onion in food processor. Skim fat from liquor and return to a boil. Add chopped meat and liver. Bring to a boil and add cornmeal, sifting it slowly through fingers to prevent lumps from forming. Cook slowly for 1 hour. Pour into ungreased loaf pan and let cool. To serve, cut into slices and fry in oil.

A traditional Della Robia wreath hangs on a shuttered door.

Turnip Hash Browns

The turnips have a somewhat sharper flavor than potatoes, which gives these hash browns a unique twist.

3 large turnips
1 Idaho potato
1 egg
1/4 cup bacon fat
Salt and pepper

Peel turnips and cook in boiling salted water about 10 minutes. Drain and cool. Peel and grate potato. Grate turnips. Place potato and turnips in bowl and season with salt and pepper. Beat egg and add to turnips. Mix together by hand. Form into 1-inch cakes and sauté over medium heat until golden brown.

Iron Skillet Country Omelet

For a different flavor, try using a good white cheddar or smoked gouda in place of the goat cheese.

12 large eggs	3 cups zucchini
1/4 cup heavy cream	1/2 cup leeks
1 teaspoon salt	1-1/2 cups red bell peppers
1/2 teaspoon pepper	1/4 cup olive oil
2 cups red bliss potatoes	6 ounces goat cheese
1 red onion	

Preheat oven to 400 degrees. Whisk together eggs, cream, salt, and pepper. Set aside. Slice potatoes and onion thinly. Chop zucchini, leeks, and peppers. Heat oil in skillet. Add zucchini, onion, and peppers and sauté lightly. Remove vegetables from skillet, drain, and set aside. Add potatoes to skillet and sauté. Add egg mixture to skillet and place in heated oven for about 2 minutes. Spread vegetables on eggs. Bake about 5 minutes, until just about set. Crumble goat cheese on top. Bake about 5 minutes more until puffed.

A country omelet is a filling brunch dish.

Smoked Chicken Hash

Fresh chicken can be substituted in this dish, but cook the chicken first and add about a cup of chorizo or andouille sausage and a dash of cayenne for flavor.

3 pounds smoked chicken
4 cups potatoes
2 cups onions
1 cup green and red bell peppers
2 teaspoons salt
2 tablespoons olive oil

Cut chicken and potatoes into 1/4-inch cubes. Chop onions and peppers, toss them with the salt, and sauté in olive oil until soft. Add the potatoes and cook until they start to brown. Add the chicken and cook for a minute or two. With the back of a spoon, flatten the mixture and cook until bottom is brown and crisp.

*H*E IS OBLIGED TO COME HERE FOR TWO MONTHS EVERY WINTER.

Dolley Madison

Blackeyed Peas with Ham Hocks

You can make a traditional Hoppin' John by adding one cup of rice to the ham and pea mixture and simmering for about 20 minutes.

1 pound dried blackeyed peas   2 tomatoes
1/2 pound ham hock   6 cups water
1 large onion   1 teaspoon salt
1 bay leaf   1/2 teaspoon pepper
                                      Dash of hot sauce

Sort and wash peas. Cover with water and let soak about 8 hours. Wash ham hock. Trim fat off ham hock and render in large pot over medium heat. Chop onion, add to rendered fat, and cook until transluscent. Drain peas and add to onions. Add bay leaf, cover with water, and simmer for 45 minutes until peas are nearly tender. Remove ham hock and pull meat from the bone. Dice meat and return to peas. Chop tomatoes. Stir tomatoes, hot sauce, salt, and pepper into peas.

BLACK-EYED PEAS WERE SOWED BY FARMERS TO SUPPLY NITROGEN TO THE SOIL. THE FARMERS DIDN'T HARVEST THEM FOR ANYTHING, SO EVERYONE WAS ALLOWED TO PICK THEM. THEY WERE SO PLENTIFUL IN THE FIELD THAT WE NEVER PLANTED THEM IN THE GARDEN.

Edna Lewis

Goblets belonging to President Zachary Taylor are set on a walnut drop leaf table surrounded by 1720 Queen Anne chairs.

Cinnamon-Orange French Toast with Burnt Orange Syrup

The longer you soak the bread the better, as it will become the consistency of custard. When it cooks, it will puff up like a beignet.

12 large eggs
3/4 cup sugar
3 teaspoons cinnamon
4 cups half-and-half

1/4 cup orange juice
1/4 cup Grand Marnier
16 thick slices French bread
1/4 cup vegetable oil

Beat eggs and sugar together. Add cinnamon and mix lightly. Add half-and-half, orange juice, and Grand Marnier. Soak bread in mixture for at least 1 hour. Heat vegetable oil in large oven-proof skillet until hot. Sauté one side of each slice of bread until nicely browned. Turn bread over and place skillet in 450-degree oven for about 15 minutes until puffed and nicely browned on both sides. Serve with burnt orange syrup.

Burnt Orange Syrup

1-1/2 cups sugar
1 teaspoon lemon juice
1/4 cup water
1 unpeeled orange, thinly sliced
1/4 cup Grand Marnier

Combine sugar, lemon juice, and water in small saucepan. Cook until caramelized and dark amber in color and mixture coats the bowl of a spoon. If sugar crystals form, carefully remove from sides of pan with pastry brush that has been dipped in water. Remove hot caramel from heat and add orange slices. Return caramel mixture to heat and add Grand Marnier carefully as mixture will flame. Cook about 5 minutes until mixture is thickened. Strain mixture and let cool.

Reveling

The custom of making noise to usher in the new year goes back to ancient times when it was thought a great deal of shouting, wailing of horns, and pounding of drums would drive evil spirits away. The practice of blowing trumpets at midnight has been practiced in many countries around the world for centuries. In Britain, in order to emphasize the ringing in of the new year, bells were muffled until midnight when they could be rung loud and clear to signify that the new year had arrived.

Antebellum Virginia was no exception. New Year's Eve was a very noisy time. However, while the Northern states celebrated with bells, horns, whistles, drums, and even pots and pans, Virginians turned to gunpowder to provide the proper noise for the new year, thus setting a fashion for the South to mark the new year with firearms. As the clock struck 12, gentlemen would raise their guns and shoot and children would shriek in glee while the women put their hands over their ears. When a neighbor caught the echo, he would answer by firing, as did his neighbor, and so on. The custom was followed enthusiastically throughout the Old Dominion, and soon became the official way to usher in the new year.

Visiting Day

On New Year's Day, planters typically rang in the new year with an "at home" or open house. Thought to have begun in New York, the tradition spread southward in the late 18th century. George Washington held an "at home" after the Revolutionary War, and John Adams brought the custom to the White House where it remained until after the Civil War.

From the 1840s until the end of the 19th century, Southern ladies remained at home on New Year's Day to receive gentlemen, who paid social calls on as many of them as they could on a single day. The visits often began in the morning as the gentlemen had many calls to make before the day ended.

The "at home" was literally a holiday from the rigid formality usually expected at the plantation. It was a gala time. Men in silk hats flocked in pairs throughout the day, leaving cards and partaking of eggnogs and cordials. No invitations or replies were necessary. Everyone was welcome. And everyone was expected. There were enormous feasts set out for everyone who dropped in. The sideboard was laden with cakes and eggnog. Bonbons and cornucopias filled with nuts were scattered throughout the rooms. And there was always whiskey or brandy available for those gentlemen who felt that they could not face one more cordial or eggnog.

It was considered a slight for someone to neglect to call. So at the end of the day, the cards were counted and comments were made about who had failed to appear.

The parlor is ready for New Year's Day callers.

Carrot Muffins

This also makes the most delicious carrot cake. Just pour the batter into two 8-inch cake pans and bake at 350 degrees for about 35 minutes. Top with cream cheese icing.

2-1/2 cups all-purpose flour	1 cup vegetable oil
1-1/2 teaspoons baking powder	3 eggs
1-1/2 teaspoons baking soda	3/4 cup milk
1 teaspoon cinnamon	1-1/2 cups grated carrots
1/2 teaspoon salt	1 cup chopped pecans
1-1/2 cups sugar	

Preheat oven to 425 degrees. Oil or spray muffin tins. Sift together flour, baking powder, baking soda, cinnamon, sugar, and salt. Add pecans and mix well to cover. Add oil. Beat eggs and add to mixture. Add milk and carrots and mix lightly with wooden spoon. Scoop into muffin tins. Bake for 20 minutes.

I REMEMBER HELPING TO THRESH THE WHEAT AND TAKE IT TO THE MILL TO HAVE IT GROUND INTO FLOUR. THE FLOUR ALWAYS TASTED OF WHEAT BERRIES. REFINING WHEAT WAS A NEW PROCESS BACK THEN, AND ONLY THE WELL-TO-DO COULD AFFORD IT.

Edna Lewis

Raisin Bran Muffins

You can keep this batter covered and refrigerated for up to three weeks and scoop out muffins to bake as you need them. Just be sure not to stir the batter or it will collapse and the muffins will be like lead.

2-1/2 cups flour	2 tablespoons grated orange peel
1 teaspoon salt	
3 teaspoons baking soda	2 cups buttermilk
1-1/4 cups sugar	2 eggs, beaten
1-1/2 teaspoons cinnamon	1/2 cup vegetable oil
3/4 cup raisins	3 cups raisin bran cereal

Preheat oven to 425 degrees. Oil or spray muffin tins. Sift together flour, salt, baking soda, sugar, and cinnamon. Add raisins and mix to coat well and distribute. Add orange peel, buttermilk, eggs, and oil. Mix lightly with wooden spoon. Do not use mixer and do not over mix. Fold in raisin bran cereal. Spoon into muffin pans. Bake for 20 minutes.

Old-Fashioned Tea Biscuits

Tea biscuits were a favorite on Sunday mornings in New Jersey. We like to think Dolley had them when she visited her uncle there.

3-1/2 cups cake flour
2 cups all-purpose flour
3 tablespoons baking powder
1 tablespoon salt
4 ounces cream cheese
1/4 cup unsalted butter
1/4 cup shortening

3/4 cup sugar
4 large eggs
1 tablespoon vanilla
2 cups sour cream
1 cup dark raisins
1/4 teaspoon vegetable oil

Preheat oven to 400 degrees. Grease two baking sheets. Mix the flours, baking powder, and salt into a bowl and set aside. Cream the cream cheese, butter, and shortening. Beat on high speed for 2 minutes. Gradually add the sugar. Add 3 of the eggs, one at a time. Beat until creamy and light yellow. Add the vanilla. Alternately add flour mixture and sour cream. Add raisins and stir lightly just until mixed. Dough will become tough if over-mixed. Roll or pat dough out to a 2-inch thickness. Cut into biscuits. Whisk remaining egg and oil and brush on the tops of the biscuits. Bake for 12-15 minutes until tops are shiny and golden.

Welcoming pineapples are handmade from dried roses.

Twelfth Night Ball

The holiday season, which began December 24 and lasted until January 6, was the height of the social season on the Virginia plantation. In antebellum Virginia, it was not uncommon for guests to arrive unannounced and for their visits to last the entire 12 days. But the highlight of the season was the last day, or Twelfth Night.

Though not well-rooted throughout the colonies, Twelfth Night was celebrated extensively in Virginia. Primarily a religious holiday, Twelfth Night signified the Wise Men bringing gifts to the Christ Child. It was also customary to exchange gifts. And, since it marked the beginning of the carnival season preceding Lent, it was the perfect time to throw a party. It was the last of the merrymaking before beginning the preparation for spring plowing and planting.

In true Virginia fashion, an elaborate ball supper is served. Beautiful appointments are the focal point of the

An 18th-century dining room is appointed with the most elegant holiday finery.

evening's festivities. Garlands adorn windows, stairways, and chandeliers. Fine damask and lace dress the tables. And serving dishes of fine porcelain, sterling silver, and crystal are brimming with food.

A silver epergne holding fruits, nuts, and sweetmeats takes center stage on the highly polished dessert table. A fresh fruit ring surrounds bowls of cakes, trifles, and syllabubs. Trays of tarts are complemented by a cornucopia spilling fruit onto the table. A large King Cake awaits the lucky person who draws the prize. And on a sideboard, a silver samovar and porcelain cups are ready for tea while stronger drinks fill crystal decanters in the nearby spirits room.

Bloomsbury

Looking at Bloomsbury as it stands today, it is quite evident it once hosted many social gatherings. The first floor features a spirits room and a charming ballroom known as the Great Hall. Overlooking the hall is a musician's gallery large enough to accommodate a spinet and two violin players. And legend has it that violins played to accompany dancing of "roundels" on the lawn in the summer. Thus, it is obvious this solitary outpost of Colonial Virginia served the purposes of the dancing and festivities in a family which apparently enjoyed entertaining.

Today, romance and history continue in Bloomsbury, the ancestral home of both James Madison and Zachary Taylor. This original manor house had been out of the family estate for 175 years. So, when the late Jaquelin Taylor was able to purchase this quaint Queen Anne cottage as a wedding gift for his bride-to-be, dreams came true. Challenged with its state of disrepair, the Taylors spent the next 20 years restoring this 18th-century jewel.

Built in 1722 by Colonel and Mrs. James Taylor II, the great-grandparents of the two Presidents, Bloomsbury is said to have been the furthest house west of the James River. Today, it stands as the oldest house in what eventually became Orange County. But, although Col. Taylor and his wife, Martha Thompson, created their small plantation on the very cutting edge of the frontier, they nevertheless brought with them some of the graces of their heritage.

Bloomsbury is an unusual design and construction for so small a structure. The roof line incorporates a porch that may be the earliest in Virginia. Made at the site, the basement and chimney brick of the original structure are laid in English bond, a 17th-century technique unusual for the 18th-century and unique to Orange County. Virtually all of the 18th-century interior and exterior woodwork, as well as hardware on the doors and cupboards, survive intact. Although the gardens have not been restored, indentations of the sunken garden can be seen to the rear of the house. Ponds flanked both sides of the property and numerous outbuildings surrounded the manor house.

No other Queen Anne house of this period in Virginia shows more sophisticated or ingenious design under such limited circumstances. It has been beautifully furnished with the 17th- and 18th-century collection assembled by Mr. and Mrs. Taylor. The collection reflects not so much a period 18th-century house as a remarkable dwelling that has welcomed Jefferson Davis, Generals Lee and Stuart, and—of course—James and Dolley Madison.

Twelfth Night Ball

Menu

Champagne Cocktails

Roasted Eggplant Soup with Rosemary

Creamed Oysters and Country Ham with Corn Cakes

Endive and Mache Salad with Goat Cheese Straws

Black Currant Tea-Smoked Duckling with Five-Spice Port Wine Sauce

Hominy Patties

Matchstick Winter Root Vegetables

Dessert Buffet of

White Chocolate Cheesecake with Raspberry Coulis

Tyler Pie

Dark Chocolate Pistachio Terrine

Chestnut Pudding

Praline Maple Mousse

Old-Fashioned Trifle

Plantation Coffee

Dolley's Fashions

Once she was married, Dolley discarded her somber Quaker dress and indulged in fancier tastes. She loved to shop and began buying stylish clothes. French fashions were the rage, and she chose the finest with little regard for popular fads. She became partial to the Empire style dress with its short sleeves, low revealing neckline, high waist, and clinging fabric. It was a style that older women thought vulgar and indecent. To emphasize her beautiful neck, shoulders, and arms, she modified the designs by raising the neckline.

At an open house held after Madison's inauguration as President, Dolley wore a long white Empire style dress with a train of finely woven cotton. Her bonnet was made of purple velvet and white satin with a white feather. At the ball that evening, she dazzled everyone in a buff-colored velvet dress with a long train. A matching turban topped with bird-of-paradise feathers was on her head.

Turbans became her signature, appearing as part of nearly every outfit. But whatever the event, Dolley's fashions stole the show. At an elaborate New Year's Day Open House, Dolley wore a yellow satin dress embroidered with butterflies and a turban made of feathers. For a February reception, she wore a rose-colored gown with a train of white velvet lined with lavender satin and edged with lace. On her head was a white velvet turban embroidered in gold and topped with ostrich feathers. Another party saw her in a black velvet dress trimmed in gold and a tiara set with sapphires replacing her usual turban.

A reproduction of a dress Dolley Madison wore is on display at Montpelier.

Roasted Eggplant Soup
with Rosemary

This soup is so delicious that it is even loved by people who profess to dislike eggplant. Be sure to use fresh rosemary. It is a major contributor to the flavor.

3 garlic cloves	2-1/2 cups chicken stock
2 large eggplants	1-1/2 cups heavy cream
3 tablespoons olive oil	1/2 teaspoon rosemary
1/4 cup thinly sliced shallots	1/4 teaspoon black pepper

Preheat oven to 400 degrees. Peel and chop garlic. Put on flat sheet and roast in oven for 2-3 minutes until lightly brown. Split eggplant in half and coat pulp with some of the oil. Lay oiled side down on baking pan. Roast in oven until tender. Scoop out pulp and discard skins. Heat remaining oil in saucepan. Sauté shallots until tender. Add roasted garlic and eggplant. Cook about 2 minutes. Add stock and return to boil. Add rosemary. Cook about 15 minutes. Purée mixture in food processor. Add cream and blend. Strain and transfer to saucepan. Reheat and correct seasoning.

*M*ADAME … DECORATES HERSELF ACCORDING TO THE FRENCH IDEAS, AND URGES ME TO DO THE SAME.

Dolley Madison

Champagne Cocktails

This old-fashioned drink is fun for special occasions. Be sure to use sugar cubes as the bitters sizzling on the sugar cubes is what makes this drink.

8 cubes sugar
16 dashes bitters
48 ounces chilled champagne

Place one sugar cube in the bottom of each champagne glass. Saturate the sugar with bitters. Fill the glass with champagne.

Butterfly plates dating from the 1600s adorn a Classical Revival mantle.

Creamed Oysters and Country Ham with Corn Cakes

Oyster and ham pie is a very popular dish in Virginia. The corn cakes in this recipe are a nice change from the doughy crust usually associated with this dish.

THESE CORNCAKES ARE YET ANOTHER WAY OF MAKING BATTER BREADS OUT OF CORNMEAL, WHICH HAS BEEN A FAVORITE IN VIRGINIA SINCE I WAS A CHILD. THE TANGY FLAVOR THE CORNMEAL GIVES THE CAKES IS FURTHER EN-HANCED BY LETTING THE BATTER SIT OVERNIGHT.

Edna Lewis

For the corn cakes
1 cup white cornmeal
1/2 teaspoon salt
2 teaspoons baking powder
2 eggs
2/3 cup milk
2 teaspoons melted butter

For the oysters
2/3 cup slivered country ham
1 cup heavy cream
1 cup oyster liquor
1/8 teaspoon cayenne pepper
2 tablespoons butter
30 large oysters

Mix cornmeal, salt, and baking powder together in a bowl. Beat the eggs in a separate bowl, add milk, and stir well. Add milk mixture to the cornmeal mixture and mix thoroughly. Cover bowl and set in refrigerator for at least 8 hours. Remove batter from refrigerator and allow it to return to room temperature. Mix well and stir in melted butter. Spoon batter onto a hot, greased griddle to make small pancakes about the size of a silver dollar. Set aside, keeping warm. Briefly sauté ham in butter and drain.

In a medium saucepan, reduce heavy cream to half and set aside. Place oyster liquor in a small saucepan and reduce by half over medium heat. Add cayenne pepper. Strain the reduced liquor into the cream. Set aside, keeping warm.

Fold oysters into warm cream mixture and cook over moderate heat just until the edges begin to curl. Stir in ham. Stack corn cakes and spoon mixture on corncake stacks.

The unique English spinet dates from 1695.

Endive and Mache Salad

Mache, also known as lamb's lettuce or corn salad, grows wild in the cornfields. Its leaves are tender with a tangy, nutlike flavor. It is very perishable and should be used within a day or two after purchase.

For the dressing
2 tablespoons apple cider
  vinegar
1/4 cup walnut oil
1/4 teaspoon salt
Pinch of pepper

For the salad
1 small head curly endive
8 heads mache

For the garnish
1/4 cup black walnuts
3 tart red apples, sliced
Goat cheese straws

Combine vinegar and walnut oil. Add salt and pepper. Toss endive in dressing. Arrange on serving plate. Center mache bouquet on top. Sprinkle with chopped black walnuts. Arrange apple slices and goat cheese straws around lettuce bouquet.

WHEN THE FIRST TURKISH MINISTER . . . ARRIVED IN TOWN, A GRAND BALL WAS GIVEN IN HIS HONOR TO WHICH THE BEAUTY AND FASHION OF THE TOWN FLOCKED.

Dolley Madison

Goat Cheese Straws

1/4 cup butter
1/2 cup goat cheese
1 cup all-purpose flour
1/2 teaspoon salt
1/4 teaspoon cayenne pepper

Preheat oven to 350 degrees. Combine butter and goat cheese in bowl of food processor. Add salt, cayenne, and flour and pulse until mixture resembles cornmeal. Place on floured board and knead. If mixture seems dry, add a bit of water; if mixture seems wet, sprinkle with flour. Roll out to 1/8-inch thickness and cut into strips. Place on greased cookie sheet and bake 5 to 8 minutes or until golden brown.

Endive and mache salad with goat cheese straws makes an elegant presentation when served on an heirloom Thun Behemian plate.

Black Currant Tea-Smoked Breast of Duckling

If you don't have a smoker, a regular grill will work just fine for smoking the duck.

Beautifully cooked duck is presented on heirloom Bohemian porcelain.

4 quarts black currant tea
Black currant tea leaves
8 duckling breasts
1 tablespoon black pepper
Salt
2 garlic cloves, crushed

Cover wood chips with 2 quarts black currant tea. Add the tea leaves and let soak for 24 hours. Set duck breasts in a large pan. Combine remaining tea, pepper, salt, and garlic, and pour over duck. Put pan in refrigerator and let ducks soak about 8 hours. Remove duck from liquid and drain. Place charcoal in a smoker, light, and allow to burn until mostly gray. Fill water pan and spray grill with vegetable spray. Shake water off wood chips and add wood chips and tea leaves to hot coals. Place duck on grill inside smoker. Close lid on smoker and let smoke for 1 to 2 hours. Add more chips as necessary. To serve, bone breasts and put on grill or in oven for a few minutes to finish cooking and heat through.

Five-Spice Port Wine Sauce

1/3 cup brown sugar
2/3 cup port wine
1/2 teaspoon five-spice
1 cup beef stock
Salt and pepper

In a saucepan caramelize sugar. Add port wine and spices, cooking over low heat until sugar dissolves completely. Add stock and cook over low heat until reduced by half. Season to taste.

Hominy Patties

Cooking fresh hominy is such a time-consuming affair that we use canned cooked hominy. Be sure to wash canned hominy at least three times in cold water to remove the taste of the liquid it is soaked in.

3 cups cold boiled hominy grits
2 tablespoons butter, melted
1/3 cup grated Romano cheese
2 eggs, beaten

Milk
Flour
Salt and cracked black pepper

Add melted butter to hominy and mash fine. Add cheese and mix well. Add beaten eggs and enough milk so that mixture can be molded into patties. Dredge in flour and sauté in butter until lightly browned.

WE HAD HOMINY MORE OFTEN THAN RICE WHEN I WAS GROWING UP. ALTHOUGH TRANSFORMING CORN INTO HOMINY WAS A LONG AND TEDIOUS PROCESS, IT WAS SO DELICIOUS THAT IT WAS WELL WORTH THE EFFORT. IT WAS ALWAYS SERVED AT BREAKFAST WITH GRAVY SPOONED OVER IT.

Edna Lewis

Matchstick Winter Root Vegetables

The celery root, salsify, and leek elevate this dish beyond the usual steamed and buttered carrots.

4 carrots
4 salsify
4 celery roots
1 large leek
Olive oil for sautéing
Salt and pepper

Peel and slice carrots and salsify. Cut into small matchstick-like pieces. Wash leeks well and cut greens off one inch above white part. Cut into matchstick pieces. Sauté in olive oil until barely tender. Season to taste.

The Frascati dining room is decorated in holiday splendor.

Tyler Pie

Everyone in the South has a favorite recipe for Tyler pie. This one was adapted from an old Orange County recipe that has been praised for its perfection.

W E HAD THIS PIE WHEN THERE WEREN'T ANY BERRIES OR FRUIT IN SEASON. SINCE IT USES STAPLE INGREDIENTS AND IS EASY TO MAKE, IT HAS ALWAYS BEEN AN EVERY-DAY SOUTHERN PIE. IT IS SIMILAR TO A CHESS PIE AND IS NAMED FOR PRESIDENT TYLER SINCE IT IS SAID THAT HE AND HIS RELATIVES WERE FOND OF IT.

Edna Lewis

2 eggs
1 cup sugar
1/2 teaspoon flour
1/4 teaspoon salt
1/2 cup butter

1/2 teaspoon vanilla
1/2 teaspoon grated lemon zest
1 cup milk
1 pastry-lined pie pan

Preheat oven to 350 degrees. Beat the eggs. Mix sugar with flour and salt and add to the eggs, mixing well. Add butter, vanilla, and lemon zest. Stir well and add the milk, mixing well. Pour into pastry-lined pie pan. Bake for about 30 - 35 minutes until set and golden brown.

Dark Chocolate Pistachio Terrine

Although this terrine looks and tastes like it took hours to make, it is really quite simple to prepare. Try topping it with the raspberry coulis.

2 pounds semisweet chocolate
1 cup heavy cream
2 tablespoons brandy
1/2 cup pistachios, shelled

Cut chocolate into small pieces and place in mixing bowl. Add cream and place bowl over simmering water until chocolate is melted. Remove from heat and add brandy and pistachios. Pour into a 1-quart mold and refrigerate at least 8 hours. Serve with fresh whipped cream.

White Chocolate Cheesecake

The addition of the raspberry coulis makes this creamy cheesecake a lush, elegant dessert.

For the graham cracker crust
20 graham crackers
1 tablespoon sugar
1/4 cup butter, melted

For the filling
10 ounces white chocolate
1/2 cup heavy cream
16 ounces cream cheese
4 eggs, separated
4 teaspoons vanilla
Pinch of salt

Preheat oven to 325 degrees. Combine graham crackers and sugar in food processor. Pulse until fine. Add butter. Process until well blended. Butter a 12-inch springform pan and press mixture evenly over bottom and sides. In double boiler over simmering water, melt white chocolate. Add heavy cream slowly and stir until smooth. Remove from heat and cool slightly. In a separate bowl, beat cream cheese until smooth. Add egg yolks and blend well. Add melted chocolate, vanilla, and salt. Beat on medium speed for a minute or two. Put egg whites in a separate bowl. Beat until soft peaks form. Fold into chocolate mixture. Pour into crust. Put in oven and bake for 55 minutes. Turn off oven and let cake stand in oven for 1 hour. Remove and let cool.

White chocolate cheesecake is creamy and sinfully rich.

Raspberry Coulis

2 cups frozen raspberries
1/2 cup sugar
1/2 cup water
1/2 cup fresh raspberries

Defrost raspberries and purée in food processor with sugar and water until mixture is smooth. Strain. Garnish with fresh raspberries if available.

King Cake

The delicious and festive King Cake is baked in honor of the three kings. Made with rich Danish dough, covered with a poured sugar topping, it is decorated with typical Rex colors—purple, green, and gold—signifying justice, faith, and power. A plastic baby is baked inside the cake. Tradition has it that the person who gets the doll is required to continue the festivities by hosting another King Cake party.

The tradition began in Europe centuries ago. It was used to signify the Feast of the Epiphany—or Twelfth Night—when the wise men brought gifts to the Christ Child. People all over the world celebrated Twelfth Night by exchanging gifts and feasting. Since Twelfth Night is the beginning of the carnival season that ends with the beginning of Lent, parties abound.

Today, Twelfth Night parties are not as popular as they were years ago. However, the King Cake is still the preferred dessert during Mardi Gras in New Orleans. Brought to this country by French settlers, Mardi Gras is the final celebration before Lent begins.

Chestnut Pudding

Serve this with whipped cream and sweetened chestnuts for a wonderful holiday dessert.

1-1/4 cups boiled chestnuts	1 cup sugar
2 teaspoons sugar	2 teaspoons rum
5 eggs, separated	1 cup whipped cream

Mash chestnuts and mix with 2 teaspoons sugar. Slightly beat the egg yolks with 1 cup sugar. Beat egg whites until stiff. Fold in the egg yolk mixture, the rum, and the chestnuts. Grease a pudding mold and sprinkle with sugar. Pour chestnut batter in mold and place in a hot water bath. Steam for 1 hour. Remove from bath and let cool. Unmold and top with whipped cream.

Maple Praline Mousse

The crunch of the pralines mixed with the smoothness of the mousse is an unforgettable taste treat.

For the pralines	2 cups half-and-half
1 cup sugar	1/2 cup golden brown sugar
1 cup chopped pecans	1/4 teaspoon salt
	4 teaspoons maple extract
For the mousse	2 cups whipping cream
1-1/2 envelopes plain gelatin	

Put sugar in a heavy skillet and set over medium heat until it begins to melt. Do not stir, but be careful not to let it scorch. When sugar is melted and a nice amber color, add the pecans. Stir and pour into lightly buttered dish. Let cool. When cold and hard, crush into pieces. To make the mousse: Place gelatin in a bowl and spoon about 3 tablespoons half-and-half over it. Stir together and let soften for about 5 minutes. Put remaining half-and-half into a saucepan and heat until scalding. Stir together brown sugar and salt in medium-sized bowl. Slowly whisk in hot half-and-half. Add softened gelatin mixture and whisk until completely dissolved. Stir in maple extract. Place bowl in larger bowl of ice water and stir occasionally until mixture thickens slightly. Beat cream until soft peaks form. Do not beat cream stiff. Fold maple mixture into cream until blended. Spoon into soufflé glasses and refrigerate until set. Just before serving sprinkle pralines on top.

Old-Fashioned Trifle

*This trifle can be enhanced with fresh berries in season. Just slice and
sugar the berries and put on top of the custard.*

6 eggs, separated
1/2 cup sugar
1-1/2 tablespoons lemon juice
1-1/2 tablespoons orange rind
2 tablespoons sherry
1 cup cake flour
1/2 teaspoon salt
1/4 cup dark rum
1 cup currant jelly
1/2 cup blanched almonds

For the custard
4 eggs
4 egg yolks
1 cup sugar
2 tablespoons cornstarch
3 cups half-and-half
2 teaspoons vanilla

*A typical trifle in a crystal
bowl is surrounded by crystal
compotes and vintage figural
glass ornaments.*

Preheat oven to 350 degrees. Beat egg
yolks until thick and lemon colored.
Beat in sugar, lemon juice, orange rind,
and sherry. Beat until foamy. Sift flour 3
times and fold into egg yolks gently but
thoroughly. Beat egg whites until foamy.
Add salt and beat until stiff but not dry.
Fold into yolk mixture. Bake in a springform pan for 60 minutes. Invert pan on
rack and let cool. While cake is cooling,
make custard. Beat eggs and egg yolks
until light and creamy. Beat in sugar,
cornstarch, and half-and-half until
blended. Transfer mixture to a heavy
saucepan and cook over moderate heat,
stirring and whisking constantly until
mixture comes to a boil. Lower heat
slightly and cook, stirring constantly, for
about 2 more minutes. Whisk any
lumps that may form. Remove from heat
and whisk in vanilla. Place pan in a
larger bowl of ice water and stir occasionally until cold. Slice cake horizon-
tally into 4 pieces. Sprinkle one-quarter
of the rum over each of the slices. Put 1 slice into an attractive
glass bowl. Spread top of slice with currant jelly and spoon one-
quarter of the custard over the layer. Repeat with the next 3
layers. Garnish top with blanched almonds.

Banana Syllabub

Traditional syllabubs, popular in the 18th century, were made with wine, but we have updated it to something we found more appetizing.

3 very ripe bananas
3 teaspoons superfine sugar
12 ounces light rum

3 ounces Cointreau
6 ounces lime juice
3 cups whipping cream

Slice banana and put in bowl of a food processor. Add sugar, rum, Cointreau, and lime juice. Blend until smooth. Whisk the cream until it just begins to thicken. Then beat in the banana mixture until the cream holds its shape. Spoon into wine glasses or champagne flutes. Chill well.

The duPont breakfast room at Montpelier is decorated for the hoidays in true Edwardian Victorian fashion.

Plantation Coffee

The secret to making a delicious hot drink is to use fresh ground coffee and freshly whipped cream.

8 ounces boiling water
12 ounces Southern Comfort
4 ounces Amaretto
24 ounces fresh brewed coffee
8 tablespoons whipped cream
8 teaspoons white creme de
    cacao
2 teaspoons crushed almonds.

Preheat 8 coffee mugs by swirling an ounce of boiling water in each. Discard water. Add Southern Comfort and Amaretto to freshly brewed coffee. Pour 5 ounces into each cup. Top each cup with 1 tablespoon whipped cream. Drizzle creme de cacao over top. Dust with crushed almonds.

Index